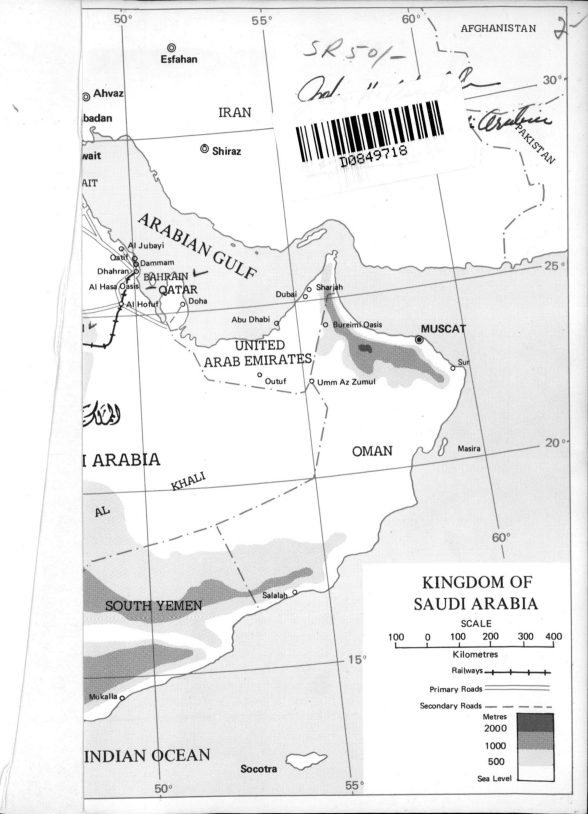

50° 55° 60°

AFGHANISTAN

SR50/-

D0849718

⊚ Esfahan

⊚ Ahvaz

IRAN

badan

30°

⊚ Shiraz

PAKISTAN

wait

AIT

ARABIAN GULF

25°

○ Al Jubayi
Qatif ○ ○ Dammam
Dhahran ○
BAHRAIN
Al Hasa Oasis ○ QATAR
○ Al Hofuf ○ Doha

Dubai ○ ○ Sharjah

Abu Dhabi ○

○ Bureimi Oasis

MUSCAT ⊚

Sur ○

UNITED
ARAB EMIRATES

○ Outuf ○ Umm Az Zumul

ARABIA

OMAN

Masira

20°

KHALI

AL

60°

SOUTH YEMEN

Salalah ○

Mukalla ○

INDIAN OCEAN

Socotra

15°

KINGDOM OF
SAUDI ARABIA

SCALE

100   0   100   200   300   400

Kilometres

Railways ╶┼─┼─┼╴

Primary Roads ═══════

Secondary Roads ─ ─ ─ ─

Metres	
2000	
1000	
500	
Sea Level	

50° 55°

Faisal

The King and his Kingdom
by
Vincent Sheean

1975

University Press of Arabia

Published by
University Press of Arabia
1 West Street, Tavistock, England
Printed and made by Butler & Tanner Ltd.

Contents

Author's Foreword

KING Faisal of Sa'udi Arabia has emerged in recent years as a central figure not only in countries of his own language and tradition but in the world at large. This can hardly surprise anybody who has watched his development for any length of time, since he early showed and always maintained the reflective and contemplative habit of mind which tends towards wisdom. He was ready for his part when history summoned. It is easy to say that in a world ever more thirsty for crude petroleum the sovereign of a country owning the greatest reserves of that substance must have increasing importance, but we have only to think of a few others (such as this King's own older brother Sa'ud) to realize that such is not the case. The man himself must be equal to his task. It involves a consciousness every Arab prince does not possess.

For Faisal was, after all, born in an Arabia torn by tribal feuds and rivalries often turning into war; he was only the third in line of succession to what was then a minor throne. It was the commanding genius of his father to change all that: to unite the greater part of the Arabian peninsula for the first time since the Prophet Mohammed (Upon Whom Be Peace!) and to give his clan name of Sa'ud to the whole kingdom which came into being when Faisal was a young boy. His development since then has kept pace with that of his country. Often he has been criticized by extremists for his moderation, but he is distinguished above all by a keen sense of what can and what cannot be done, as well of what ought to be. Who could have expected such restraint, such knowledge of the way of the world, and such astute political intelligence in the true sense (without benefit of 'intelligence service') to be there when they were needed? They were there. Faisal either had them innately—which the doctrine of Mao Tze-tung decries as impossible—or they developed in him by experience working upon a truly remarkable material.

This book is an attempt to trace the main lines of that development. Originally my own interest in the new kingdom and its creator (whom we in the west always called 'Ib Sa'ud' from the clan name of his whole dynasty) was aroused early, very early indeed. I had in fact studied the Wahhabi movement, the origin of it all, from Ferdinand Schevill at the University of Chicago before it had conquered its kingdom, and wrote a term-paper of some length on the subject (although materials were scanty) along about 1920, at a time when most of the western imagination was preoccupied by a quite different dream of Arabia—that of T. E. Lawrence. My interest was maintained through the years, and on one or two occasions I attempted to go to the new kingdom of 'Ibn Sa'ud' (Abd el-Aziz is his correct Arab name). Unfortunately it never was possible; the old King distrusted writers and journalists in general and visas were hard to get, nor were there Arab offices abroad from which to obtain them until the 1940's. In 1960 I was at last able to go down from Cairo, through intervention by my old friend Azzam Pasha, founder of the Arab League.

It was then (May, 1960) that I first met Crown Prince Faisal, who is now King, and obtained some sharp impressions of his original and decisive personality.

(These were published in the United States and elsewhere by the North American Newspaper Alliance.)

Readers of this book (if such there be!) may wonder why I state here, in the beginning, something which is told later in its context. It is to make clear at the outset that mine is no recent interest in Arab affairs; that I have felt it since schooldays, and that it has been fed by many visits to Arab countries through the years. It plays an important part in my book *Personal History*, widely read before the second world war. To be accused of being 'pro-Arab' seems as natural to me as it was to be 'pro-Jewish' in the era of Hitler. Never at any time after my first visit to Jerusalem have I been 'pro-Zionist'. The distinction between these terms seems to be incomprehensible to most Americans, in particular, and to many in other countries as well. They do not see that the deepest sympathy for Jews under malevolent persecution *as Jews* is by no means contradictory to sorrow for those Arabs who have

vii

been driven from their homes to make room for a Zionist state, or sympathy for those other Arabs who are determined to defend their countries and their lives against any further expansion of that experiment. In short, I am both pro-Jewish and pro-Arab, but never pro-Zionist, and it is this which makes it so difficult to be heard at all on the subject in the United States.

The Crown Prince (as he was in 1960) did not seem to question this viewpoint, nor have other Arabs in great positions. They cannot exactly share it: the thing is too close, too urgently a matter of self-preservation.

But Faisal ibn Abd el-Aziz there and then seemed to me an Arab equal to the task of leading his band of peoples into some kind of reconciliation of their internal disputes in defence of their land against an alien and expanding state in their midst. That is and could only be expansionist; it may be by 'creating facts' (as General Dayan says) or, more simply expressed, by grabbing and holding, but the expansion-ism is integral to the idea of Zionism. In my earliest days in Jerusalem no attempt was made to conceal it. The extravagances of Jabotinsky and his followers, who preached a 'Jewish empire from the Nile to the Euphrates', enjoyed a good-humoured tolerance in official circles, and although it was never the professed Zionist doctrine there was left little doubt in my mind that it was in fact the aspiration at the base of Zionism. It is implied in the very notion of 'the gathering-in of the exiles', as the revered Zionist leader Ben Gurion put it, according to which every Jew anywhere in the world was an exile from that state a-borning. Is it strange that inhabitants of the neighbouring countries favoured by such attentions (Arabs or whatever they might be) would take alarm? Divided and ill-informed as they were, beset by personal, clan and dynastic rivalries, they were one in language and ethnic tradition—even if not racially one, as few peoples are—they possessed their own summing-up of the Judaeo–Christian–Islamic religion native to them, and in their eyes it was the only true mono-theism; they had been attached to this land for thousands of years, perhaps in part aboriginally (Frazer and Toynbee both thought so). To lead such quarrelsome fragments into some kind of union based on their firmest realities was a task awaiting somebody who could both see and create. I thought Faisal was that man. The cross-currents of personal ambition did not affect the matter much; slaves of any ideology could neither think nor see straight; Gamal Abd el-Nasr (known in the west as Nasser) was self-made and ever-desirous of augmenting the job; but Faisal was born where he was. Most of all, he was there at the right time, and history had provided him the means of assuming leadership. His ambitions were not for himself but for his people, all of them.

Having thus convinced myself of the truth of his mission I found, on my return to Cairo, that the discovery had been made some time ago by the finest Arabs of my acquaintance. The lamented George Antonius was no more, but many of his closest friends (such as Azzam Pasha, then high in influence and power) had already become convinced adherents and so remained through the 1960's when Nasser's illusory meteor dazzled much of the Arab world. This has only been accentuated with the events since then: Nasser's adventurism resulted in the 1967 war, so disastrous to the Arabs, and after Nasser's death a more moderate wind prevailed over the whole area he had influenced. Along with all of this the world's thirst for petroleum became almost insatiable—both in 'advanced' and 'backward' countries—just when the wells of Arabia were increasing their yield at a dizzying pace. It was impossible for King Faisal not to occupy, as the 1970's wore on to 1972 and 1973, that position for which nature and circumstance had intended him, that of leadership in a newly conscious Arab world. Unity there was not, but there existed a growing feeling that the entire region had long been cheated of its due and was still (after the departure of imperialism and even of disguised colonialism) being cheated by the real technology and the self-asserted superiority of the western countries in particular. Then came the various Arab agreements of 1972–73, in which King Faisal played a decisive part. Arab petroleum had been and was being poured into the war machine of the state of Israel, and it was on this point, rather than on the worldwide consequences of economic action, that the agreements concentrated. By the mere fact of being one world indeed, or at any rate one planet, the consequent rise in prices in the industrial countries was followed by devastating slumps in the less developed lands which had also learned to depend heavily on all the petroleum they could get. The outlook is still far from bright, but at least in some countries, such as the United States, where the Arabs had scarcely even ranked as human beings before, a change of attitude (not unmixed) took place.

Through it all the King has preserved his slow and moderate course, generally under attack from his own extremists as well as from opponents. His age and the plague of constant ill-health for decades has made his task always harder and the hours of his day ever more burdened than before, but he has come through with at least a beginning of justice for the Arab peoples that could have been no more

A*

than a dream in the 1920's. To this he has added an attention to all Islam—whether in accord with his own doctrinal heritage or not—equalled by few in modern times: never has the annual pilgrimage to Mecca been more important or more impressive in the Muslim culture, since Faisal is the Custodian of the Holy Places and cannot for one moment forget it. Perhaps it is as a religious phenomenon above all that he will take his place among the elders of his faith. He is much too modest to make any claim to the wisdom which has come to him through much experience and many turns of fate, but it is acknowledged in him by visitors from afar as well as by those who come under his sway. A Muslim from a distant land who has worked with him for years says that if a republic took the monarchy's place tomorrow Faisal would be elected President; and another from outside his realms has told me that service to his country and religion (in whatever capacity) would be, in such a case, his only desire. Nothing of the kind is likely to happen, but to be so regarded by close fellow-workers is not frequent in the courts of power.

This King, his family and kingdom, and the distinctive religious impulse from the heart of the desert that produced them, brought this book into being. Scholars and Arabs themselves may do far better, but none with a better will.

1   The Destiny

1

WITHIN a wedge of mostly barren land, swept by the bitterest winds and burned by the hottest sun, all the great religions of the western world have had their birth and early development. How it happened must be forever a matter of conjecture, since there seems nothing in the climate, races or collective experience of the long, narrow triangle between Mecca, Jerusalem and Damascus to make its inhabitants different from others who have equally toiled, feared, hoped and worshipped. The awe-inspiring desert is there, of course, and there is something in Renan's remark that monotheism is 'the religion of the desert'; and yet the desert has been there all through known time, both historically recorded and archaeologically reconstructed, and the area so fertile in faith is not substantially different from other deserts in the Arabian peninsula or above. Nor is the population in any important respect different from its kindred to north and south. The hard winters and cruel summers are the same for leagues in all directions; the desiccation and barrenness do not change; the rocks and sand are the same, the meagre food for men and beast does not vary across an immense, monotonous tract; and why one small, particular segment of this vast near-nothingness should have produced such exalted examples of religious genius, powerful in the consciousness of mankind for many, many centuries, is possibly the most unanswerable conundrum in a history filled with puzzles.

The answer given by each of these three great religions, Judaism, Christianity and Islam, is the same; that is, that the fountain of truth was nothing less than divine revelation. Even if this were quite literally true, accepted, as it is by countless millions all together, we still are left with the sense of awe and wonder that so *much* could have been revealed, over so many ages of time, in the same neighbourhood. The Hebrew law and doctrine is maturely expressed in the fifth book of the Pentateuch, known as Deuteronomy; it is thought to have been written about six hundred years before the Christian era; and from that to the Prophet Mohammed (Upon Whom Be Peace!) there passed over a thousand years of constant religious aspiration, assertion and speculation, including the eclosion of Christianity, and all, or substantially all, connected with this same hard-tried, long-suffering and inhospitable corner of the earth.

And even this thousand years, of course, is only a final phase into which centuries of experiential preparation lead as many roads may lead to a city. Nobody knows how old the great shrine of the Kaaba at Mecca may be. It was certainly a very ancient place of worship and pilgrimage long before the day of the Prophet. Islam believes it to be 'the House of Abraham', just as Abraham was 'the first Muslim', and hence there is a rooted belief among Muslims that it in some way is the original shrine of monotheism. Scholars say there is 'no evidence of any historical connection' between Abraham and the Kaaba; what 'historical evidence' there could possibly be I do not know, but anyhow the origin of the tradition or legend, whichever it is, is lost in the mists of the past. Certainly the introduction of gods and goddesses from afar—from Egypt and the Orient, or from simple animistic symbols—had been going on for a very long time by the time Mohammed was born, and a kind of complicated polytheistic paganism ruled the holy centre. This and its many abuses, its 'abominations', were the spur to his genius, fired him with the rage that destroyed them.

By Islamic time, dating from Mohammed's journey to Medina in 622 A.D. (the Hijra), the population of the peninsula and its neighbouring regions was no longer homogeneous, if it ever had been. Paganism of one kind or another predominated—in the desert tribes it was of the animistic variety, it seems—but there were other beliefs and some non-Arab elements. Jews and Christians existed in the cities or towns and even among the tribes. There were Jewish–Arab tribes even in the peninsula, Arab-speaking nomads distinguished from the others by their adherence to the Jewish religion. There were Christians scattered through the whole area by now, too, and most of the early converts to Islam in Syria and the north were such: Arabs by race and language, Christians by religion but often oppressed by their Greek

(Byzantine) masters. There was obviously a fluidity of population on the trade routes and a kind of racial kinship between the predominant Semitic elements, precluding sharp national divisions in the modern sense and leading toward some kind of common ground, some shadow of an unexpressed unity. It was left to our own century —the Cairo Settlement of 1922, in which Winston Churchill as Colonial Secretary sorted out the war-time promises and drew the map which obtained general acceptance—to make separate 'nations' with fixed frontiers. It is a characteristic of 'the Arab world', as most Arabs call it, that nationhood is still a rather relative term: a citizen of one Arab nation feels himself to be at home—rightfully—in all other Arab countries, and the obstacles which contemporary political alignments throw in the way of this freedom are resented. Unity has never been achieved through all these centuries, but it has never ceased to be a possibility (whether dream or hope) which sometimes came near and often seemed remote indeed, too remote for definition.

Most powerful of the influences towards unity, aside from the Arabic language which is intertwined with it, is Islam, the faith of the Prophet Mohammed; it has prevailed over all others in the middlelands, those between the Mediterranean and the Indian Ocean, for a good many centuries. (There are important Christian pockets; other minorities subsist; there are even Islamic sects which seem far from the Muslim intent; and yet the general fact of an Islamic majority, amounting in some areas to unanimity, always remains.)

Our wedge of sand and rock, birthplace of so much in the religious consciousness, was also where Mohammed was born, lived and died. This was in the seventh century after Christ (that is, after the year fixed upon by the Romans after Constantine as being that of Christ's birth). Mohammed was a new Prophet, the last of the august series, who is regarded by his followers as being the messenger of God.

2

He was born in Mecca of the Koraish, a ruling clan associated with the care of the Kaaba. The date generally accepted for his birth is 570 in the Roman Christian era, which remains the time conventionally current in the west (and many other regions) today. From then until his death in 632 of the same era, his life was almost all exposed to the light of history, and it has often been remarked that he is the only one of the great prophets of whom this is true. There is, at any rate, proof for the important moves of his mission after 610 A.D.

The Jewish and Christian influences which appear plainly in the Koran must have been absorbed in the environment of his youth, somehow, whether in Mecca or elsewhere. He had heard the Old Testament, of which Islam accepts the first five books, the Pentateuch, as revealed truth from which the Jews had wandered away; the Four Gospels of Christianity are accepted in the same manner. There were certainly Jews in Medina, Christians in Mecca and Medina both; there may have been some early influences of which we know nothing. The Prophet was probably illiterate—'an unlettered messenger to an unlettered people'—but the point is disputed and probably always will be. (Some of the most devout Muslims I know are convinced that he could neither read nor write.) Yet Arabic scholars for centuries have marvelled over the beauty of his language, which evidently remains, to this day, unrivalled. In a sense he invented the language (as Dante did Italian) in a form subsequent centuries have found unapproachable.

Literate or not, he certainly received no formal education, and may well have formed his literary genius by listening to those 'poets' (narrative singers for the most part, as in ancient Greece) who flourished in Arabia. He was, as has often been said, a migrant, as were almost all other young males in the time and place, and went on journeys to Damascus with the caravans. His principal employer was a widow Khadijah, whom he married when he was twenty-five and she was forty. It was a monogamous marriage—this in a country where polygamy was at the time unlimited—and a very happy one. It was only after Khadijah's death that the Prophet, in his last years, contracted polygamous alliances (one was Christian and one Jewish) which sometimes may have been as much for political advantage as for other reasons.

It was around his fortieth year that he began to have visions and hear voices. He used to go off into the hills to be alone and meditate, and here the voices came to him. It was obviously some time before he dared to communicate to others—and then under severe admonitions—what his voices told him, or even whence they came. He was a poor man of relatively no importance in Mecca, even though he did belong to the ruling clan of the Koraish—it was like most clan relationships (as in the Scottish Highlands, for instance) in that the poorest might be cousin to the richest. Mohammed had no prepared audience, no gathering of predisposed listeners. When he did speak it was to humble folk, and his earliest followers were among slaves and vagabonds, as happened with his predecessor, Jesus. He had never written down the words that came to him, as he understood,

4

from the Archangel Gabriel; perhaps he could not write them; and it was left to others to get these revelations into order as the Koran. The canonical order of the lessons or chapters had been adopted and the entire work written down before his death.

There seems no question that during this period (around 610 A.D. and for another six or eight years) Mohammed was without a fixed plan or design. He was called 'the poet' in his native town, he was not taken seriously by the authorities, and he had himself no tremendous urge to convert the unbelieving, so far as appears. What made him into a flamelike preacher and teacher of his own truth was the steady degeneration of his own clan and people in Mecca, who were by now indulging in every excess of polytheistic idolatry known to the time. (Muslims believe today that this was in degeneration from the monotheism of Abraham; even if there is no evidence, it is still the belief.) Gods and goddesses of strange races, effigies from afar, sticks and stones of obscure meaning, were set up in the city for worship, even in the Kaaba or probably especially in the Kaaba. Along with these abominations, as the Prophet called them, there was a moral laxity growing upon the people, and the abuse of women and slaves, the extreme license afforded to polygamy, the errors of greed and envy (usury, for instance, and cheating) scandalized the land. Against all this the Prophet was compelled to speak up as strongly as he could in the supreme sense of his mission, the oneness of God.

And so, insensibly, during the years 615–620 or thereabouts the poet and visionary who had been viewed by the rich Meccans with good-humoured contempt gradually became a scourge to the city. We do not know just when the rulers of Mecca began to see the danger (to them) in this fiery preacher to whom voices spoke in his own home now as at first in the wilderness. He had probably acquired a number of believing followers before the grandees of the town began to notice. And although many of these followers were poor and obscure, they also included some men of note and intellect such as Abu Bakr, eventually the Prophet's father-in-law, who was to become the first Caliph of Islam after Mohammed's death.

The culminating power of the preacher had become such that his liberty and perhaps his life itself were in grave danger, and it was then that he took the decisive step: he left Mecca, accompanied only by Abu Bakr, on a swift journey (or 'flight') to the town of Yathrib, some two hundred and eighty miles to the north, where he had friends and clansmen. This flight, famous in history as the Hijra, is

5

the beginning of the Islamic era, and the town of Yathrib has been renowned through the centuries as Medina—The City. Mohammed lived there for eight years and it was there that most of the structure of Islam came into being, either in the Koran itself, as written down by the disciples, or in various sayings of the Prophet which were recorded (or merely remembered and passed on orally) by those who knew him. The opportunities for invention and adornment were obvious, and in the next few centuries a jungle of legend grew up around the words which were repeated, in steadily decreasing authenticity, as being transmitted through the generations from the Prophet and his Companions. Like Christianity and Buddhism, both abounding in myth and invention, Islam gave rise to an epigonic literature during the earlier centuries which had in time to be restrained and in part discarded.

None of this was the direct responsibility of Mohammed. He was in his last years called statesman, warrior and conqueror, even though his realm was small, his ambition limited, his military actions few and on a small scale. Twice he beat off invading forces from Mecca and at last, in the western year 630 (the eighth after the Hijra), he captured Mecca itself and made his monotheism supreme.

The Prophet's military force was small—never more than about a thousand men—and he achieved this triumph through the doctrine and the faith it inspired. This doctrine was simplicity itself; it was pure monotheism, first and last. The one God was the be-all and end-all of the Prophet's religion. That he was the messenger, the human and limited messenger, of that one God, and that his direct utterance (the Koran) was divinely inspired, followed upon his whole earthly work. (To the theologians it was also divine in the sense of eternal, pre-existing.) In life he seems to have been merciful and compassionate (those words with which he begins and ends every lesson) as well as, in general, humanly kind. His terrible severity was occasional and was directed to the enemies, as he saw it, of Islam. He was tolerant of the other religions 'of the book', as he called them (Judaism and Christianity) unless they conspired against him. There are many stories, all no doubt apocryphal from the point of view of scholarship, which show his good nature and benevolence; of unknown origin and often regional character, they do show, by their dissemination through the centuries among illiterate tribes, a prevalent notion of his humanity.*

---

* The Roman solar year 632 is, of course, ten years after the Hijra which begins Islamic time. Islam counts by the moon, as a very large part of the world does,

In the western year 632, when Mohammed died, being at the time sixty-two years old (we think) on the solar calendar and almost sixty-four on the lunar calendar, he had made monotheism both religion and law in the holy city of Mecca, consecrated, as Muslims believe, by Abraham and Ishmael, fathers of the northern Arabs. Medina and Mecca and the land between, almost three hundred miles, were his, and Islam was already making rapid headway among the Arab tribes of the open desert. His was still a very small world in comparison to what it was so soon to become. He had fully enunciated his doctrine in the Koran, which was at least written down by many followers during the last years of his life. Few poets and visionaries have made the subsequent action, the deeds which are their result, unfold so naturally and seem, as these do, to arise from some inner inevitability.

In an incredibly short space of time the religion of Mohammed spread through the desert and on upwards into the Byzantine Empire in the north and Persia to the east: it had its conquests by the sword and by the book, but the readiness of the populations to receive it counted for an immense amount—that, and the feeble but ferocious internal quarrels of the Christians. Half a world was Islamized and to a considerable extent Arabized before most of the conquerors had time to draw their swords.

There were reasons, many and various, aside from the appeal of the Messenger. A true believer had economic and social advantages (much relief on taxes, for instance) and, regardless of race or origin, had equal opportunities with all the rest of the faithful. From the very beginning, there was some kind of natural democracy, a fundamental egalitarianism of spirit or feeling, which did not seem to flourish in other faiths. Most of all, the faith of Mohammed was persuasive then, as it is today, by its utter and complete simplicity. If you believe in the one-ness of God and reject all heathen or pagan practices, and if you confess that Mohammed was God's messenger to mankind, you are a Muslim: no more is needed. To a world which

---

and the years in the two systems are obviously not of the same length. Every thirty-two sun-years provides about an extra year of time in the moon-calendar, and thus it turns out that the year 1964 A.D. was approximately 1384 A.H. There have been an extra forty-two years thus accumulated since the Hijra. Visitors to Arab lands have observed the difference chiefly in religious holidays and commemorations, which are a little earlier every year than they were the year before. For convenience in communications most Islamic countries follow the solar calendar today (along with time marked off from Greenwich) but the old system is still used for most purposes in Sa'udi Arabia.

had been substantially ignored by the Jews (exclusive and familial, then as now) and bewildered by the Christians with their complicated theology, there was an irresistible attraction in the faith of Mohammed. The Jews had little to offer anybody who was not born within their family; the Christians had little to offer but puzzles and riddles about three gods who were separate but identical. A world athirst for mono-theism—as all worshippers must essentially be, since the essence of divinity is its high union, its aboveness—could find nothing so clear, simple and true as the essential statement of Mohammed.

That—not the sword—was the reason for Islam's conquest of so very large a part of this world in so short a time.

3

Egypt and all North Africa were taken by the Arabs and their con-verts (or adherents) within fifty years of the Prophet's death: the Islamic hordes had reached the Atlantic Ocean by 683 A.D. Early in the next century it was Spain's turn, and one of the most flourishing Islamic dynasties was set up there by an Omayyad refugee prince, in a golden age for centuries and in a long decline for others, until it ended in 1492, the year of the discovery of the New World. All through the Middle Ages mathematics, astronomy, philosophy and the higher learning in general (including the works of Aristotle and Plato, Jews and Christians and even remoter thinkers along with Arabs) were encouraged in the Arab courts, particularly at Cordova and Baghdad, the two extremes of a loosely allied empire. The Ottoman Turks from deeper Asia were converted to Islam and swept westward in the fourteenth century, finally capturing Constantinople and the last vestiges of the Byzantine Empire in 1453. It was this eclipse of the remaining Greek culture in the east that added to, with its flood of refugees towards Rome and the west, that revival of classical interest which we call the Renaissance. Possibly if there had been no Renaissance there would have been no Reformation—it is this integument of thought and act, this web of consciousness, which makes history beyond exact computation. It is the apparent accident— or, in Arab terminology, the will of God—that is supreme, not only in the smallest sequences but in the greatest of events. Arabs and Arabism declined with the advance of the Ottoman Turks. It was inevitable. From the seventh to the fourteenth centuries the Arabs had been friendly to all the digestible races, tribes, nations and religion in their path. They had welcomed adherents. This was,

8

indeed, their strength. It is hardly possible to find enough material or military reasons for their fantastic success. Even today we know why Rome conquered the Mediterranean world, and there have been monumental works (such as Mahan's *The Influence of Sea Power Upon History*) to show us how it worked. No such examination of the Arab advance has been possible since so much of it does not yield to analysis.

The Ottoman Turks, on the other hand, were without mystery. They had numbers, weapons and fanatical bravery: they had adopted the faith of the Prophet Mohammed without any of its implications or overtones, its mercy and its compassion. The Turks were a material people if there ever has been such a thing. They wanted chiefly loot. For quite a space of time they got it, and whether it was at the expense of the Arab, Jew or Christian (these indissolubly intertwined peoples and faiths of the tortured middle-lands) made little difference.

As a result, or as a part of the general results of such a barbaric invasion, the Arabs became a subject people—like the Greeks, like the Slavs of the Balkans and like the Berbers of North Africa. It is true that the Arab tribes and even their city-dwellers, by and large, fared better than the Christians and Jews, merely by virtue of having been the people of Mohammed. Even the most ignorant Turk was aware that Mohammed was an Arab. Indeed, since the Turks had no alphabet, no grammar, and no history, they tended to adopt what they could from the Arabs through the years after the conquest. Even so, although they treated the Arabs badly, they tried to give their whole attitude in this respect an air of religious comprehension or even fellowship.

To me the documents which most vividly show the temper and quality of Turkish rule in relatively modern times are the novels written in Greece and the Balkans during the present century. They are closest to us in time and sense; they ring true because they are fresh from memory (memory from perhaps only the father or the grandfather, but redolent of truth) and because most of their significant facts can be easily proved. These are, for example, the novels of Nikos Kazantzakis in Greece, of Ivo Andric in Yugoslavia, and even the stories of Panait Istrati in Rumania. Of these, it would appear to me that *The Bridge Over the River Drina,* by Ivo Andric, gives the clearest, plainest and coolest account of Turkish rule that I have read. *Freedom or Death,* by Kazantzakis, lacks the elevation of Andric as its author lacks the Croatian's intellect, but it is also a remarkable evocation of days when death itself often seemed preferable to Turkish domination.

Still, the pattern is nowhere the same as anywhere else. Parts of the Arabian peninsula never did yield to the Turk—although maybe because the Turk never bothered to take them over. From Gibraltar to Aden there were all sorts of variations on imperialism with numerous degrees of autonomy amounting almost to independence. The 'Barbary states' of North Africa (Morocco to Tunisia) were never really subject to the central rule of Constantinople after the seventeenth century. Under their Turkish viceroys or pseudo-Arab sultans they evolved into something about the same as independence, and their official piracy was the last of its kind at sea. (The United States, under Thomas Jefferson, made a successful war upon them for the protection of shipping—strange footnote to a weird story.) Egypt, the largest dependency of the Ottoman Empire, fell under the viceroyalty of a single family during the nineteenth century and thus attained a kind of separateness which was never again to be impaired. *Asia Minor* (an expression now fading into disuse) was physically divided into administrative units and governed from Constantinople, actually by appointed Turkish officials, who often rotted into a kind of habitual sovereignty in their places.

On those parts of the Ottoman Empire where there was a Turkish population (Anatolia, for example) the government was not as oppressive or greedy as in the places where most people were Arabs or Christians. So far as Asia Minor is concerned—the present-day Middle East with the exception of the Turkish provinces from Smyrna to Soviet Armenia—the Turks were disliked and had every reason to distrust and fear their subjects. No rebellion took place here on any scale in the nineteenth century because the subject populations—referring always to Asia Minor or the Middle East—were themselves as lazy and indifferent as the Turks, subject to the same lethargic acceptance of fate, and materially a little bit behind their masters in weapons and techniques. (The machine-gun, however primitive, is always a bit ahead of the spear.) In other words, the Arab Muslims, Christians and the Jews were torpid, venal and ignoble in a torpid, venal and ignoble age.

The Christians of Slavic and Greek race in Greece and the Balkan peninsula were quite otherwise inspired and led. They revolted against the Turks about every ten years or so throughout the nineteenth century and always made a formidable showing, even though they were suppressed by greater force (accompanied by atrocious massacres) in the end. Every time they failed they aroused the emotions of Western Europe and Russia. The Tsars of Holy Russia during the nineteenth century, under the original mystic impulse imparted by Alexander I, felt themselves to be protectors of the Greek Orthodox Christians and somehow imparted to all the imaginative youth of Russia some kind of pro-Balkan enthusiasm, as is reflected in the Russian literature of the time.

These Greek and Balkan aspirations, although they had bitterness, sorrow and death for their reward, were bound to win in the end, as they did. The Arabs watched it all with a mixture of feelings. First of all, they could not hope for the victory of Christians over Muslims, even though they may have felt the Turks were not altogether Muslim, but opportunist. They could not hope for the victory of the Turks over the Christians either; the Turks were their enemies, the destroyers of their land and people, but at the same time the Turks were the defenders of Islam against the infidel, and in fact the Sultans of Turkey had for several centuries called themselves 'Caliph', successor of the Prophet. This was a complicated affair, and during the nineteenth century—which extends also to the year 1914 of the twentieth—there was, along with stagnation, exhaustion, poverty and despair, a certain sheer xenophobia among Arabs, a feeling that all foreigners (Muslim or non-Muslim) were their enemies, that the Turks and the Christians and Jews had alike conspired to reduce them to the uttermost depth of misery and humiliation.

Even the Jews, parents of Christianity and Islam, began to stir with a new vision of activity in the nineteenth century. The Viennese journalist Theodor Herzl had evolved a notion, not precise legalistically, that some or many Jews should make settlements in Palestine (by agreement with the Turks) and thus evoke the Old Testament as authority for a geographical centre. The idea caught on amazingly during the last decade of the nineteenth century and the beginning of the twentieth. A great number of intelligent men began to believe that if you endowed a religion with a geography you could make it a nation. Settlements in Palestine began to flourish under various endowments (by permission of the Turks). A general world-wide benevolence began to shine upon these settlements as being rectification of an ancient wrong. The Arabs were only vaguely aware of the possibilities of the Zionist movement, as it was called (Zion being the name given to the land of origin during the Babylonian exile). To this day many Arabs do not know what the word Zion means, and many more do not know the difference between a Jew and a Zionist.

However, in the period during which the Ottoman Empire was falling apart and the Arabs stood still, both the Jews and the Christians fought and won a fair number of battles. The Balkans really emancipated themselves, although the power of Russia (more threatened than used) played an enormous part in their success. The western democracies, England and France, as usual found themselves on the wrong side, by which I mean the side opposite to that which they essentially believe in and belong to; the United States and Japan were still in embryo; China was paralysed and the papacy had not yet established any relationship with modern times. Most European nations regarded themselves as being islands of egotism, caring nothing what happened to any other so long as they could eat and sing.

But the Arabs, who formed the greatest part of the population of the Ottoman Empire and had no reason to love the Turks, were thus faced, in the war of 1914–1918 (once known as the 'Great War') with a dilemma. The reigning Sultan had declared (in his capacity as Caliph of Islam) a holy war against the British and French. The whole Islamic world was asked to accept this, although it is quite obvious that the Sultan had succumbed to the combined threats and bribery of the German Empire as well as his own exaggerated admiration for the German Emperor, Wilhelm II. The 'holy war' (*jihad*) was never accepted by the Arabs. It is true that there were many Arabs in the Turkish armies, some of whom reached high rank, but the Germans and Turks never fully trusted them. Anybody will be treacherous if he is daily forced to serve that which his innermost being rejects.

This was the opening which the British Arab Office in Cairo, under General Gilbert Clayton, tried to extend as a way of winning (or helping to win) the war. Their aim was to get the Arabs, hither and thither and yon, to rebel against the Turks and do enough damage either to knock Turkey out of the war or to make that country useless as an ally to Germany.

One of the young officers from the Arab Office, T. E. Lawrence, was sent down to Arabia with some sacks of gold to see if he could suborn, entice or subvert the Sharif of Mecca, Hussein, or any or all of his sons and relatives, into a campaign of attack upon the Turks.

He found, as must have been expected, an old-fashioned awe of the Turks (who had ruled the Arabs, *these* Arabs, for five centuries) along with a fear of machine-guns, artillery and hand-grenades. Sharif Hussein wanted a vast amount of support before he would engage upon such an enterprise, and he also wanted (not being stupid) some guarantee of what the Arabs might derive from their efforts after the war was over. T. E. Lawrence did not himself promise anything, so far as we know, and his subsequent agonies of conscience towards the Arabs (that he had 'betrayed them', for instance) were nonsense. He bore his messages back to Cairo and there followed from Sir Henry MacMahon (General Clayton's civilian superior) the letters which, with Hussein's replies, constitute the MacMahon–Hussein correspondence, all of which has been published many times and constituted the base upon which Winston Churchill, as Minister of the Colonies under Lloyd George, with Colonel Lawrence as his chosen and trusted adviser, drew the map of the Middle East in 1922 in Cairo.

It was cleverly drawn and it seemed to take care of all those irreconcilable promises. As a matter of fact, it was a fraud and probably Churchill knew it. It did not give to the Arabs that free and independent existence of which they had dreamed. Instead, it gave them a string of subsidiary states, subsidiary to Great Britain under the fading concept of 'the defence of India'. Faisal Hussein, the prince to whom Colonel Lawrence had so grandly entrusted the future of Arabia, was pushed off to Baghdad by Churchill; he became the first King of Iraq, a rich kingdom indeed but not to be compared with the whole empire he had been promised. He did not last long and his direct line perished. Churchill and Lawrence made Faisal's older brother, Abdullah, Amir of Transjordan, a country which had not existed up to then and is always in danger although Abdullah's grandson, the present King Hussein, gives it a sign of life. Old Hussein and the rest of his family faded from history, and the victory of the Sa'ud family over Mecca and the Hejaz in 1924 brought even their long supremacy in the holy cities to an end. Abdullah's grandson, the brave young King Hussein of Jordan, is the last member of the Hashemite dynasty to remain in power, threatened though it is from all directions.

T. E. Lawrence, a writer of amazing gifts, has given in *The Seven Pillars of Wisdom* his own account of the Arab uprising against the Turks and his part in it. Even the facts in that narrative have been much disputed, and it seems likely to remain in literature (not in history) as a work of art and the revelation of a tortured soul. To my mind this he was, anyhow, and even if he had never seen an Arab it would have been so; but everybody who deals with this subject has to face, sooner or later, the fact that Lawrence played a great part after the war was over through his advice to Churchill. He never accepted Zionism; Churchill did, with a good deal of romantic rhetoric. (I have personal knowledge of his style in that matter.) Lawrence was evidently trying to get all he could for the Arabs, and in particular for the Hashemite family to whom he felt himself bound by the wartime loyalties. He never seems to have been aware of the vital part the Sa'ud family, rivals from the other side of the peninsula, were to play in the development of Arabia. His limitations of temperament were worse than his intellectual obstinacy, and although he did help to create the pattern of the Arab states in succession to the Ottoman Empire, it was to seem to him quite valueless in the end—another betrayal among so many, for which he felt strong personal guilt. It is doubtful to me if he could ever have avoided it.

And with the Zionist promise, so ill-defined and subject to progressive interpretation, along with others to the French, the conflicting promises to the Arabs stood little chance of real fulfilment. Churchill and Lawrence anointed their consciences by creating thrones for the Hashemite princes and appealing to the mandate system of the League of Nations for all their empire-building, a solution with an air both of novelty and justice. A sigh, perhaps, for the Middle East. There was nothing they could do about Arabia itself.

The Arabian peninsula has always escaped the imperial envelopment. We know that Napoleon Bonaparte had his eyes upon it, although only because it lay athwart the route to India. Even if he had no desire to conquer Arabia it would have been unwise to go ahead with his Indian dream without securing at least the Red Sea coast for his imperial convoys. The necessity vanished, as did all Napoleon's dreams of eastern empire, at the Nile—the battle of Abukir, 1798—and sea-power once more proved its supremacy on the largest scale.

Indeed in the nineteenth century, which was in many historical respects the century of the British navy, there was no necessity to worry about any intervening land mass (Arabia or any other) unless it presented distinctive reasons of its own for attention. Once they had acquired Aden—with various other protectorates along the south coast—the British had no need to worry about the huge desert peninsula, which could neither harm nor help them in their imperial concerns. Ships could go (after 1866) from Suez to Aden without even noticing Arabia. The huge, sparsely inhabited desert, offered few temptations to even the most insatiable empire-builder of any nationality, and indeed geography had removed it from the path of the late-flowering conquerors who came at the end of the nineteenth century (France, Italy, the German Empire) to claim their 'place in the sun'.

So the peninsula as a whole was spared the imperial experience. The Turks administered, in their fashion, down to the Jordan and the Hejaz, with some garrisons on the Persian Gulf as well, but the main part of the peninsula was untouched by them. There was nothing to loot in the greater part of the vast land; the tribal system was incomprehensible, with constant violence and blood feuds; the hardships even of the most peaceful life were innumerable, and no Turkish officer relished an assignment beyond Damascus or Jerusalem. (An exception was always the time of annual pilgrimage to Mecca, when there were thousands of innocent pilgrims to fleece of their possessions.)

An idea of how hard life was in the desert may be derived from a considerable number of books, even today, but the classic of an earlier time was *Travels in Arabia Deserta*, by Charles M. Doughty, first published in 1888. To my mind Doughty, with his arrogant insistence on his Christianity and his open scorn for the beliefs of his Arab hosts, was an unpleasant character, and I wonder that the perils to his life, which form a large part of his story, were not more numerous or more decisive. He travelled, roughly speaking, from Damascus to Meda'in Saleh, where he was the first European to draw and describe the Nabataean ruins; thence (often going back and forth over the same ground) to Hail, the capital of the Rashid family, and thence across the broad desert, by Boreyda and Aneyza, to Jiddah, the port of safety. The journey is described in tremendous detail and there is no doubt of its veracity and power: to this day it has not been surpassed in its field. I have never been able to think of it as 'the greatest' of all travel books, as did T. E. Lawrence, or even as 'one of the greatest', as did Edward Garnett: it is too full of the cross-grained, quarrelsome, cantankerous nature of its author, and to my mind too crabbed and idiosyncratic in style, to make that sort of appeal. But there is no doubt that the life of the caravan and the village is in it, and although much has changed (electricity is almost everywhere now, and roads and telephones and airfields) there must be still a fundament of truth in all that Doughty relates. And anybody who reads *Arabia Deserta* will understand quite easily why the country tempted no conquerors and received no visitors.

Thus it reached the twentieth century in a state not much different from that in which it had been left ages before—isolated in its abysmal poverty, forgotten, as it would seem, by nature, God and man. It was brought back into the stream of general life only in recent decades, and with a suddenness, an abrupt completeness, to which experience can offer no easy parallel. To ride the tempest of this tumultuous change without losing his Islamic destiny is the fate of our protagonist, King Faisal ibn Abd el-Aziz Sa'ud, and much in the world's future depends on how he does it.

2 The Miracle

1

THE discovery of enormous deposits of petroleum in Sa'udi Arabia in the 1930's was not wholly unexpected. Geologists and prospectors of all sorts had been on the trail of some such thing for years. Moreover the oil wells at Bahrein in the Persian Gulf, just off the Arabian coast, began to flourish in 1932 and yield a revenue which was the envy of the neighbours. The Bahrein archipelago, a British protectorate since 1861, was ruled by a sheikh who became rich as if by magic, and among those who beheld his sudden splendour with a surge of new hope there were, not only the Arab sheikhs from lower down the coast of the Persian Gulf (the Trucial States), many of whom were to share the same fate, but also the reigning king of United Arabia, a kingdom so new that it still had not grown used to its name.

Abd el-Aziz, head of the House of Sa'ud, had performed the astonishing feat of union in the space of about thirty years. This great sovereign, Faisal's father, was generally known in western countries as 'Ibn Sa'ud', or the Son of Sa'ud, although that was not his name; it was, in a sense, the name of all the sons of that house for about two hundred years, and as a family name it was finally given to the newly united kingdom (also in 1932), which became 'Sa'udi' Arabia, or the Arabia of the Sa'ud family.

The choice of the name, incidentally, was not quite so egocentric as it might seem. The new kingdom took in most of Arabia, as that word has been understood in history and geography, but with significant exceptions. The independent principality of Yemen might have objected to the use of the word 'Arabia' alone; so far as I know it did not, but there is no doubt that the states along the south coast would have been prompt to object (under their British protectorates of various dates and flavours) and there might even have been some protest from the kingdom of Transjordan (now called Jordan) which Mr. Churchill had invented to get rid of one Sherifian prince. In other words, Sa'udi Arabia might be called Arabia, but there were enough territories along its fringes to contest its right to the name. The form adopted—Sa'udi Arabia—not only indicates that it is the Arabia ruled by the Sa'ud family, but also that it does not make any claim to the territories around it.

History often affords examples of processes which, although they appear to be unrelated, come to their fruition at the same time. One of the most extraordinary of these coincidences is that the union of most of Arabia under the House of Sa'ud came at the same moment as the discovery that there were, indeed, important deposits of petroleum in that forgotten land. We shall have time to see how Abd el-Aziz united his desert kingdom through long years of struggle, both diplomatic (with the tribes) and in bitter warfare. What we remark here is that when he had completed this primary task, and was, as always, in the most desperate need of funds, there came the discovery that made everything else possible.

He was not to draw any important revenue from this source for years, because the second world war put a stop to the exploitation of the discoveries: but at least he had the certainty of a future, and after the war (beginning in 1946) the true exploitation of the new oilfields began on a scale and with an intensity Arabia had never even imagined. Before he died (November 9th, 1953) King Abd el-Aziz had already experienced the first flood of that gold which was thereafter to inundate his people and his heirs.

We should, I think, no matter how ignorant we may be (and in such matters I confess to a great ignorance), observe that the whole Persian Gulf area is what geologists call a 'large structural basin', and that such basins are known to be particularly favourable to the generation and propagation of petroleum. (I am quoting the *Aramco Handbook* here, as its expert compilers will recognize.) In fact the beginnings of the miracle came quite early in the present century, when British (and some Dutch) investigators became sure of the deposits in Persia. They did not make the big strike until 1908, and the exploitation, refinery and export date from 1912. In later years, especially in 1929, even more remarkable fields were found, and the original concession to the British (dating, in its primary form, from

1901) went through many transformations. When I first went out to Persia in 1926 for the coronation of Reza Shah (the father of the present Shah) one of the most notable guests at the ceremonies was always Sir Charles Cadman, president of the Anglo-Persian Oil Company, which had become the most important element in the life of the ancient empire. He was treated like a sovereign. That company was in part (51 per cent, later 56 per cent) owned by the British Government because Winston Churchill as First Lord of the Admiralty, during the first world war, insisted upon it. The British navy was changing from coal to oil at that moment and victory or life itself might depend upon oil.

The A.P.O.C. was the pioneer in the Middle East, and, like all pioneers, exaggerated its claims and its profits when it could. Persia became Iran, and in 1951 it nationalized the entire oil industry, bringing production to a halt. Two years later it made a new contract giving the Anglo-Iranian Oil Company (A.P.O.C.'s successor) 40 per cent of the exploitation interest and a number of big American companies another 40 per cent, with the rest divided between Dutch and French companies. (The principle of nationalization was preserved: that is, Iran owns its own fields.) The Italians and Japanese have subsequently received concessions in other areas along the Persian Gulf.

There followed a number of other important discoveries and concessions—often the concessions first and the discoveries afterwards—in the general structural basin. National suspicions and rivalries have compelled all these concessions to become somewhat more international than they once were, and in the case of Iraq the British Petroleum Company has had to give a quarter interest in the concession to the Royal Dutch-Shell, the French Compagnie des Pétroles, and the interested Americans (Standard Oil of New Jersey and Socony Mobil Oil, half). In general it may be said that the local governments of the past two decades have preferred international exploitation to that by any one power. There are numerous reasons. The British no doubt exaggerated their pretensions in the early days; they were shocked when the Americans started giving higher and higher revenues to the true owners of these lands; and if the British have now been compelled to share their concessions, or some of them, with Americans and others, it seems a natural result which they brought upon themselves. They can hardly complain: they still have a vast petroleum empire in these regions.

Of Kuwait one hardly knows what to say, except that the smallest territory seems to be the most inexhaustible. The oil concession is now shared equally by the two titled owners, British Petroleum and Gulf Oil (American), on papers signed December 23rd, 1934, extended in 1951 and expiring in 2026. The reserves there will go on for some centuries, but 2026 seems far enough ahead for practical purposes.

Those dates, by the way—the expiration of the contracts and concessions—have bedevilled me more than anything else in contemplation of this phenomenon. The big date in Persia (Iran) is 1979 plus an option for 15 years more; the big date in Iraq is 2000 for the first, with 2007 for the second and 2013 for the third I.P.C. concessions; the big date in Kuwait in 2026. When these dates fall, long after those who were responsible for them have departed, what are we to suppose? Do the engineers and technicians, the teachers and the mechanics, simply down tools and walk out, as they were forced to do in Persia in 1951? In that case production stops—unless you assume that during these next thirty years the inhabitants of the countries involved have learned all the complicated skills involved in the production of crude oil and its refinement into various forms. It is hard for me to believe that this stupendous achievement—much of which I have beheld—could be entrusted to the half-trained, and I doubt that thirty years will be enough for the Arab world to catch up with the techniques of the west in this respect.

This doubt has been conclusively proved to be foolish in many countries—India and China for two, not to mention Russia—which only a few decades ago were far, far behind the United States and England in technology. It may be so here also: we may hope. But I doubt if Arabia as a whole, or the Persian Gulf region as a whole, can produce the mass eagerness which forces young Indians and young Chinese to accommodate themselves so quickly to new techniques. To me there seem to be at least two centuries between them: those hundreds and hundreds of years of Arab stagnation make the difference.

To this my more knowledgeable Arab friends say that even today the producing countries could take over the establishment: managerial and technical skills, if it is necessary to import them, can be bought. A great part of the Aramco operation is already in Arab hands. The real difficulty, these friends say, lies in the whole field of marketing and in the refining which goes on (most of it) in market areas. Almost half the tankers of the world belong to American and European countries, which, in the marketing and refining areas, have the support of their own governments. Even when the fateful dates come, at the beginning of the next century, it is not likely that any of the oil-producing states will wish to try again an abrupt experiment like that of Iran in 1951. But so far as most of the technical requirements are concerned, Sa'udis already possess them and are using them on a big scale; that there are not more is due to the fact that such trained personnel is in short supply for the country as a whole.

However, none of these considerations affect the vaulting optimism of the young intellectuals in cities (not only in Arabia but in other Middle Eastern countries). Without ever having seen an oil well or smelled a tanker these young men calmly talk about 'nationalization of the oil industry' in ten or fifteen years. It has seemed, in listening to their talk, that they can have no idea of the complex immensity of the task. They know the oil 'belongs to the people', as indeed it does, but if it were left to the people to get it out of the earth and into the places where it is needed, nothing is likely to happen except waste and chaos succeeded (perhaps) by some interposition of a greater power. It may not be so; almost anything might happen in thirty years; but the dates are not so far ahead as not to demand serious thought.

2

The concession agreement of what is now called the Arabian American Oil Company was signed on May 29th, 1933, for sixty-six years (expiring in 1999) and an additional area was added in 1939 for sixty-six years. It covers about 340,000 square miles of Sa'udi Arabia, including offshore areas and the undivided Sa'udi half-interest in the Iraqi-Sa'udi Neutral Zone. The concession now belongs to the Standard Oil Co. of California, Texaco Inc., the Standard Oil Co. of New Jersey, each 30 per cent, and the Socony Mobil Oil for 10 per cent.

The old King, Abd el-Aziz, knew no more about this sort of thing than you and I do. He saw his neighbours getting rich; he knew in a general way that the region was supposed to be petroliferous; he was always in straits about money, which he gave away with reckless generosity even when he did not have it; and his arithmetic was rudimentary. At one point in the early thirties he is said to have cried out to his treasurer, Abdullah Sulaiman, 'Give anybody who wants them all the mineral rights for the whole kingdom for thirty thousand pounds! I want thirty thousand pounds!' At the time of the signature of the oil agreement, upon which many persons had many reserves, he is said to have said to Sulaiman: 'Trust in God and sign the agreement. We need money.' Both these stories are doubted by Arabs who knew the old King's shrewdness. A similar one was quoted by Philby more than once, but the sum mentioned was a million pounds.

Sulaiman used to keep the entire treasury of the kingdom in an iron box under his bed, and when the King demanded money he simply gave it over, or said he did not have it to give.* There were no paper records. The King's habits were lavish in the extreme. Nobody could ever know how many persons would have to be fed at any meal in his house, or any of his houses—there were always scores, sometimes hundreds—and not one person who came to see him could go away without a present. There was literally nobody refused at his palace in Riyadh, the ancestral capital, and although there may have been difficulties in the other capitals (Mecca, Jiddah, Taif) they were generally overcome, somehow or other, or the King would be furious. This scale of living was always expensive even in the days when a sheep or a goat cost one-twentieth of what is costs today. The ancestral largesse, the regal extravagance, may have seemed frightening from the point of view of any book-keeper, but there seems little doubt that it played its part in the unification of Arabia. They say there was no Bedouin in the desert who did not feel fully entitled to visit the King in his palace and eat his way through a memorable feast; and from such traditions (and assurances), when associated with a salutary justice in reserve, there arose the extraordinary power Abd el-Aziz had over the affections of the tribesmen, unmixed (under his roof) with fear.

The oil men who came into Arabia in the 1930's and made all the original arrangements were not at all familiar with Arab customs or traditions. They were mostly technical men, and Arabia was very little known in the outside world even to Arab specialists. King Abd el-Aziz, the central phenomenon, had seldom been the subject of any study by westerners: only H. St. John Philby, his lifelong English friend, had written much about him, and even Philby had much yet to do and to write. One thing that always strikes me as worthy of remark is the ease with which the Bedouin king accommodated himself to the personalities of the American engineers, geologists and

---

* Arab friends tell me this must have been pure legend, since there was no paper money and the whole treasury of gold and silver (English and Indian coinage) could not have fitted under an Arab bed. Nevertheless it was a widely quoted and printed story and I have heard it often: at least it shows Abdullah Sulaiman's personal control of the state's finance.

other technicians who came into the country in those crucial 1930's. He liked them and they liked him. Considering how little they had in common—how difficult it was for them to communicate—how remote and improbable were their dreams, how slow their progress, how difficult for the King to understand what they were doing—it is astonishing how well they got on.

'By God, I like the man's face!' he is supposed to have said after his first interview with young Mr. Barger—known as Tom Barger, now the president of the Arabian-American Oil Company. And then another thing I find most revealing from those early days is his request to the petroleum engineers: 'Could you find me sweet water?' Actually, in spite of his need of money, King Abd el-Aziz knew that sweet water, drinking water which would not make the people sick, was as important as petroleum; and the Americans (by deep wells and exploiting a spring in a nearby oasis) found the water for him.

In all these and many other ways King Abd el-Aziz showed a deep, instinctive comprehension of these newcomers from the west. He was a true son of the desert and a Wahhabi and never essentially changed, but he had an intuition which told him that these technologists, these knowers of an unknown knowledge, meant him no harm and were in fact only seeking a material truth, a reality. Why he had been less hospitable to some men of other nationalities in just those same years (or shortly before) we cannot really determine. Perhaps the Americans were so new that he tended to give them credit for new motives; perhaps the fact that the United States was so far away gave him some special confidence. And then, too, the Americans were lucky: they went to the right places: they found the oil. British and French and others had been less lucky in the period just ending. A variety of such reasons must have combined to give the King his apparent predilection for these newcomers and his willingness to entrust to them the unpredictable future that lay beneath the sands.

There must be acknowledged a certain purity (often called naïveté) in the behaviour of the American technologists which led the King's instinct to trust them. They really are, as a rule, and I have known numbers of them, primarily interested in their actual technical jobs and not in any political or international results which may ensue. This becomes obvious after a short while. It must have been far more obvious in 1932–1934 than it is today. At the present moment the Arabian-American Oil Company, which we call Aramco, is supplied with the services of some of the greatest knowers (if I may use that word instead of the misleading 'experts') on all subjects connected

B

with Arabia. If they want to know anything about Islam or its history or traditions, or what to do about a spring or a mosque or a heretical saint, or where the dissident sects have their centres, or how to reconcile opposing claims in jurisdiction, they have the men to advise them. They have an excellent library on all these subjects, right there in Dhahran, kept up to date in every respect. It is in all languages, and they have the persons, men and women, who are necessary to deal with these subjects. Their library cannot be equalled, or even approached, in Arabia, which is at present woefully deficient in that respect—but I also have discovered that some elements of their library cannot be found even in New York, either at the New York Public Library (the largest in the world, I believe) or at Columbia University. The development of such resources and such a regiment of research workers has probably taken a couple of decades at most (nothing in Dhahran is very old!) but at this present moment if a high executive of the Arabian-American Oil Company wants information on any subject—no matter how remote from oil—he can get it by ringing a bell.

This had been done by a relentless American technique which goes by various names—'personnel' is the ordinary word, 'recruitment' another—but common to all the great industrial and financial establishments so far as I know. That is, these men of power realize that they need all kinds of specialized auxiliary skills to keep themselves going. They need not only engineers, geologists, technicians of all sorts in electricity and electronics, but also professors of Arabic literature and language, and theoreticians in economics, sociology, agriculture, architecture and hydrology. I interviewed a fair number of specialists during my last visit to Dhahran, hardly any of whom had anything to do with the oil business as strictly defined. These men are obtained by a ceaseless effort on the part of Aramco to comb out the best that can be found in the American universities or in subsequent economic life which may be of service in this field. There are men of the highest intellectual attainments involved. Here we are a very long way indeed from the old-fashioned idea of the Texas cowboy drilling a hole in the ground. Aramco commands an army of specialists because it pays them well and treats them well and needs them mightily, but also (I think) because these men, or most of them, realize that they are engaged in a work which, by redeeming a part of the earth, might have a chance to redeem it all. Amongst them I have found a sense of purpose, a certainty of result from cause, a high hope for the times to come when they are no longer here. They have every material assistance in their tasks—and no theoretician or librarian or impractical philosopher is valued less because he does not extract or refine the actual petroleum. This is the newest thing about Aramco today, more astonishing, from the historical or philosophical point of view, than these ever-increasing figures of production and these staggering projections for the future.

Now, having said all this about the present day, I cast my mind back to the 1930's when a handful of men (technicians purely, knowing nothing of Arabia or the Arabs or their language or religion or culture) were breaking the ground. These American oil men had to deal with the earth and with King Abd el-Aziz, and they all understood each other. It was not possible in 1932 or 1933 for an oil man (Mr. Barger, for example, the most famous of them) to summon an 'expert' on religion or language or history or local tradition when he got into difficulty; he could not do so because they were not there. He had to do it by his own natural instinct, common sense and reflective intelligence. A process not really dissimilar, akin but not the same, must certainly have taken place in the mind and spirit of Abd el-Aziz. He knew as little about the Americans as they knew about the Arabs, but he did know that they were based too far away to desire a conquest of his country. He never could have this feeling about the British, French or any other European representative with whom his life had given him some acquaintance. Although he knew little of the world he knew men and possessed an all-powerful patriotic intuition which warned him of those who wished (or might eventually wish) to do either harm or good to his country. It was a kind of radar built into him, like the Identification of Friend and Foe (familiarly known as I.F.F.) which we used to use in the air forces, except that for him it worked better than it sometimes did for us.

Thus I am led on the evidence to think that the genius of King Abd el-Aziz, a natural and untutored genius, was the chief element in the propitious unfolding of the miracle of oil in Arabia. Fate collaborated with him. The whole pattern fell together in the most improbable way—the discovery of oil at the moment of the unification of the kingdom, for instance—but who is to say that fate is not willed or determined? At the very dawn of western philosophy Heraclitus said that a man's character was his fate, and nothing in the thousands of years since then has disproved it. Modern psychology, indeed, spends its principal effort in saying that this must, somehow, be true. To me it seems that the imperious will, the extravagant all-Arabian intertribal ambition of Abd el-Aziz, the born pan-Arabism of his soul, impelled him to seize upon every conceivable chance, and the American oil companies happened to be among them. He grasped them with the grasp which made them what they are today, the instrument of the Arab Renaissance.

3

Neither King Abd el-Aziz nor the oil companies understood for a long time what had happened. Modest sums had been paid and accepted, but it remained a gamble. We have no evidence that any large promises or prospects were given by the American oil men. Instinctively Abd el-Aziz knew that it would be big. That it would be a billion dollars a year did not cross his mind. Besides that, he had no idea of what a billion dollars might be, and neither have I. What he understood was gold sovereigns, which the Standard Oil Company of California was able somehow to obtain for him in spite of the terrible depression throughout the world and the consequent embargo on gold. The payment on signature was 35,000 gold sovereigns, counted over the table one by one to the King and his treasurer. Philby, then as always devoted to the King's interest, was actually a representative of the Standard Oil in this matter, after having had various other dealings with rival interests. It was he who advised the Americans to make their payment in gold sovereigns as being most likely to please Abd el-Aziz. The rival bidders at the time, the Iraq Petroleum Company, were ready to pay in Indian rupees (that is, in silver) which the King did not want.

The role of Philby throughout this and all the other events of Abd el Aziz's reign makes a long story, and it belongs properly to the section on that great King, where it will be found. It may seem strange that this English Arabist, converted to Islam, devoted to Arabia as he was, should have preferred American oil interests to those of England. No doubt he thought the American terms were better, their luck in general superior, their technicians more disinterested; he was against imperialism in general; and we do know that his influence in the matter was on the American side.

The whole tangle of oil negotiations and attempted negotiations during those years has paled in interest since then—after all, before the immense reality of today the tangled narrative means little. The oil strike in Bahrein (June, 1932), which was also made by Standard Oil of California under another name, was made by men who could see the great dome of Dhahran across the sea on a very clear day.

(The distance is twenty-five miles.) It is enough to say here that the urgency of coming to terms of exploring what might be there was obvious to everybody concerned, and that there were natural rivalries. When the Standard Oil won out, little time was lost in sending the first geologists into Arabia to begin the exploration.

They came from Bahrein in a launch, docking at Jubail on September 23rd, 1933. Their names were R. P. Miller (known to Aramco history as 'Bert') and S. B. Henry ('Krug'). With them was Karl S. Twitchell, one of the early negotiators, who had driven all the way across the vast peninsula from Jiddah to join them. They were entering territory which had only recently seen some bloody internecine struggles; they had been warned of fanatical xenophobia in certain regions; consequently, to make themselves less conspicuous, they wore beards and Arab clothing. They also had guides and an armed escort provided by the King.

Their first objective, of course, was what the geologists call a 'domal structure' they had seen from across the sea, which they called at that time 'the Damman Dome', since it was near the town of Damman. They were told its local name—Djebel Dhahran, the Dhahran Hill—and were encamped there for some weeks of mapping and study. This place is now Dhahran, the oil city, one of the most astonishing places to be seen on earth, where thousands of Americans and Arabs together work their complicated miracle.

In those early days, because of the ease with which oil could be certified at Dhahran, the geologists thought the whole of the concession would be the same. Working in pairs, with Arab guides and soldiers to go with them, they explored in all directions, only to find that the oil (if there was any) was too deeply buried to be detected. The 'Miocene deposits', we are told, which cover a good deal of the coast, came into existence after the geological phenomenon called 'folding' had mainly come to an end; there was also the sea of sand, shifting and impenetrable. The pairs of American geologists would be gone from their base at Jubail for five months at a time, and although they had motor transport with special sand tyres, along with plenty of supplies, their lot was certainly not to be envied. They obtained, during these arduous years, certain 'indications' of oil (that is, Eocene rocks sticking up through the sand, and other hints of a subsurface 'folding') but they were not equipped to test or prove anything: that was the job of the engineers, to come later.

Meanwhile the engineers had arrived at Dhahran, encamped on what is now the golf course, and set about their disheartening task of testing for oil. This, too, was a disappointment for a long time—from April 30th, 1935, when Dhahran No. 1 was 'spudded in', until March, 1938, when Well No. 7 proved that there was a vast field in the depths. They had to drill to 4,727 feet to get to it—a long way below what had been expected from the Bahrein and other experiences. This level or layer is now known as 'the Arab Zone' and has been enough to make all the previous disappointments rapidly forgotten. From the time of this proof, what we may call literally an abundant proof, the company began to expand rapidly, to make plans, to build houses for families, dormitories for staff, offices, and everything else that would eventually make Dhahran what it is today.

One of the things that has most impressed my ignorance is the extent to which the geologists, whom I have usually considered to be theoretical scientists, were right in almost every particular during the earliest days. Evidently the practitioners of that art—art, I should say, as much as science—can study a surface and divine, almost like a water diviner, what lies beneath it. It was shown in the whole of the 1930's that where these men said there was oil, they were right, no matter how deep the engineers had to go later on to find it. The conspicuous example is the enormous oil field of Abqaiq, which was indicated by 'clues' to two of the geologists in 1935. They did not have the instruments (structure drills, seismographs and gravity meters) which came from America in later years. The eye and the trained brain were their instruments. To me it savours of witchcraft.

The building of Dhahran after 1938 was going on a pace, and was accompanied by a great deal of dredging and mapping and exploring along the coast to find a port suited to heavy traffic. In this the British Admiralty was of considerable help, supplying charts and information in the earlier days and receiving Standard's findings later on. The company (still Standard of California, known as Socal) was heavily engaged, up to the very first year of the second world war, in what may be called, as it was in the army, 'house-keeping', the business of food, housing and the comforts of life in so far as they are possible. The bringing of families from America, slow at first, depended upon the creation of conditions they could accept; and if the families could not come, some of the best men would be lost to the enterprise. All of this complicated business was auxiliary to, but of course enormously important in, the creation of the Dhahran we see today.

Abd el-Aziz with numbers of his family, court, government and guards, to the number of about two thousand men, visited the camp for the first time on May 1st, 1939, to witness the loading of the first tanker at Ras Tanura, the site finally chosen for the port and refinery. The festivities lasted for several days, and the company put its numerous guests into 350 tents in the desert near Dhahran. It was a momentous occasion, the harbinger of a great future, even though it is doubtful if the King understood much of the procedure by which oil had at last emerged from the earth to be carried off to the markets of the world.

4

The outbreak of the war brought a curtailment of this rapid evolution. The war risks for transport were great during 1939–1943, and also it became more and more difficult to obtain supplies (technical and of other kinds) from America. The employees of the company, cut down both in number and activity, spent a good deal of their energy and resources in helping the Sa'udi government, which was equally hard hit. (They developed the oasis of Al-Kharj, for example, for water and the cultivation of vegetables, fruit and corn—a boon to the capital, Riyadh.) Every kind of convenience to which Americans are accustomed had to be curtailed during these years, and all the families had to be sent home. A change in the atmosphere became obvious in 1943, as the expanding American navy required more and more oil and the home supplies were strained. It was then that, in response to this sudden demand, the Arabian fields experienced a new rush of exploitation. At the same time the owning company was reorganized again—with the admission of Texaco, for its marketing establishments in the Far East, and an additional Standard Oil Company (New York) for participation in the vast new capital outlay now required. In 1944 this reconstructed company took the name of the Arabian-American Oil Company, shortened to Aramco, the name it has borne ever since.

It is not necessary to detail the steps in the enormous development which has taken place since 1944 and particularly since the war's end. To the surprise of many observers, there was no real slackening of demand for oil when the war was over, and although some lulls occurred in after-years for local or special reasons, there has not been a sustained slump at any time. Meanwhile the production has steadily mounted. The five years after the end of the war saw it go up twenty-five times, from 20,000 barrels a day in 1944 to half a million a day in 1949. This was accompanied by a great deal of building, offices and cottages, dormitories and electric plants, a big central air-conditioning establishment, airfields and good roads and schools and hospitals. American families of the somewhat privileged category to which these specialists belong are accustomed to many things difficult to create and maintain in the desert, but they were provided. The golf and tennis, the wonderful swimming-pools, the playing-fields, the excellent public library—all this is well established now, but it must have been a long time in the doing. To me the most astonishing thing of all, in my three visits to Dhahran (the first in 1960, the others in 1965–1966), is the grass. Every house has its grass plots, and of course this requires a prodigious amount of water. The flowers indigenous to the soil (bougainvillaea, oleander and a few others) are around the houses, and there are hedges everywhere. The hedges are decorative, of course, but the real reason for their prevalence in the residential quarter of Dhahran is that they help to keep the sand steady. Like the inhabitants themselves, the sands of Arabia are nomadic, constantly on the move, and it has been found that hedges (along with water and other rarities) help them to stay put.

If the Americans had been content to create, at God knows what expense, an agreeable place for themselves to live in the desert, nobody could blame them: they have earned the privilege by years of struggle and achievement. But they are not satisfied with that—they have been trying for years past to do what they can to help the Arabs towards a better life. Whole departments of their central organization are given over to studying ways and means of doing this, by advice or direct help, chiefly in the Eastern Province but also anywhere else where they are needed. Problems of water, agriculture, shifting sand, sewage disposal, housing, schooling and commodity supply are constantly under review. The houses they have themselves built for Aramco workers (Arabs) are models of their kind, and they have assisted in the building of some public schools also in the nearby town of Damman, where a good many Aramco workers live. You may say that with a production of well over a million barrels of oil a day (more, now, than Kuwait) they can afford all this and more. It is true. But I have seen no more startling example anywhere of a voluntary profit-sharing system which was not originally demanded or expected by its beneficiaries.* For the past fifteen years it can certainly be said that Arabs in general, Arabs of the whole country even beyond the

* There were requirements for social and technological improvement in the original contracts, but not spelled out into detail.

Eastern Province, have benefited by this phenomenon. Call it calcula-
tion if you like: but the point is, it exists. It is blatantly, extravagantly
anti-Marxian.

The prosperity of the whole Eastern Province (aside from Aramco's
own districts) has gone up with the help of irrigation, fertilization
and other projects; furthermore, Aramco not only helps the farmers
to produce but actually buys much of what they produce. The
influence of such benevolence is one of the intangibles of history.
There are many who resent the benefits they receive, and there are
many others who are grateful for them, and there are even more who
view it all with a mixture of the two, with a frosting of something
else which may be called awe or wonder. In a country where the belief
in fate or predestiny is widespread, and men of pious temperament
attribute everything to the will of God, it is clear what the prevailing
view must be (as I have had in particular from one Sheikh of the
neighbourhood): the Americans are the instruments of God's will
for the good of His own people, the Arabs.

From my point of view there is nothing wrong with this interpretation, even though I might be inclined to complicate it by other
considerations.

So the thing has come, it has flourished, it has exceedingly
flourished, and no man can truly say that it is not good. The fruits
of the earth may be so deep that only a certain category of specialists,
born beyond the sea, can penetrate their mysterious origin. The wells
of Arabia are deep, and one of them (since abandoned) was almost
15,000 feet deep, but these stubborn Americans with all their fantastic
equipment cannot be discouraged: they will go on drilling and
drilling and drilling until they have fully uprooted the secrets of the
eras past—which they have hardly touched. The most forgotten
stretches of the desert, such as the Rub'el-Khali (the Empty Quarter)
are known to be within the future exploitation, perhaps soon, perhaps
beyond anything yet experienced. In other words, this is not an end
but a beginning.

All this may sound like high praise for the Standard Oil Company
of California and its crown prince, Aramco, but it would be impossible to understand anything about the position of Sa'udi Arabia or
its sovereign without some acquaintance with these matters. Aramco
has brought Arabia (not only the Eastern Province but the whole of
Arabia) into contemporaneity, actuality, the living and vibrant
present of mankind. It has done so for profit, yes, but also out of the
boundless energy of the American technology with its constant

spilling over into the affairs of others. As is well known, the Americans can attend to their own business pretty well (at least in such matters as we see in Aramco) but that is never enough for them. They go further, they want the neighbours to have the same shower baths and television sets and air-conditioning that they have, and if they see a dry patch they want to irrigate it (whether it is theirs or not) and if there is a village without a school they want to build a school there whether it is their legal right or not. It has required constant supervision on the part of the legal department of Aramco and related ministries of the Sa'udi Arabian government (Education, Health, Interior, Agriculture, Petroleum) to keep this energumenous compassion within bounds. At the present moment I know from long hours of interviews that the desires of many Aramco benefactors (specialists who want to help the Arabs in this, that or the other particular field) are curbed by the consideration of sovereignty. They would like to dig a ditch in a village but must wait, wait, wait until the interminable train of petitions gets from the village to the provincial capital and thence, if at all, to His Majesty the King.

This is, to my mind, correct. His Majesty the King is the absolute sovereign of Arabia. Anything Aramco does must be firmly controlled by that fact. If they want to irrigate a farmer's cornfield and are not permitted to do so until they receive the royal permission, that is also correct. They have obeyed the law in their operation (in the extraction of a million and a half barrels of oil a day from the depths of an intractable geological structure) and they should also obey it in their benevolence, in their habits and impulses so far as they concern the public view, and even in their relationships with their Arab neighbours.

They do.

They obey the laws of the country in which they are working and have no objection to doing so. Prohibition, for instance—I had cocktails in only one house in Dhahran, and I truly believe it was made from an heirloom brought long ago from America. And Sunday! One night in the cafeteria-restaurant (it is both) I marvelled at the toilettes of the ladies in the restaurant or quality corner. With them were men in dark suits, although bare arms in sport shirts would have been normal. It was explained to me that this was 'Friday dinner'. I asked what that meant and was told that it meant 'Sunday dinner'. Some enlightenment was required and obtained. Under the laws of Sa'udi Arabia the Christians and Jews, when they are permitted in the country, must do their worshipping in private

32

(indeed the Jews rarely come in at all, even for Aramco), and the official, obligatory Sabbath is the Muslim Friday. In other words, Sunday is Friday. The Christians in Aramco may not care very much about their religious rites or observances, but naturally this law engaged their rebellious instincts (they are almost all Americans). Aramco explained to them that they had to obey the law of the country in which they lived, and that the best way to do this would be to pretend that Friday was Sunday. So this is what they do. They go to some kind of private service of a non-partisan nature in which prayers are said and reverence is paid to Jesus of Nazareth—perhaps like a Quaker service, I don't know—and in which the leading part is played by some Aramco man. Thus the Catholics and those born in the various Protestant sects, Presbyterian, Episcopalian and the rest, are all in the same boat on Friday, because Sunday is a working day. In other words, Friday is Sunday. Then after they get through with this morning service or worship, they go home and eat their frozen chickens from America, along with a few very good vegetables and fruits from Arabia, and sleep it off (or play games) until it is time to dress for the 'Sunday evening dinner' at the restaurant, which is on a terrace above the usual place, and thus make it Sunday. I have seen the feathers on the ladies' hats.

There is a constant misunderstanding between the Arabs and ourselves (meaning not only the Americans but others from the west) on the meaning of state property and income. It seems to us that King Abd el-Aziz, like his predecessors and successors, regarded the whole revenue of the kingdom as being part of his own patrimony, as he did other tribute or taxation. This included the oil royalties and taxes. My Arab friends insist that this was never the case and that the documents have always made it clear that the *government* was the high contracting party—not the King, not the monarchy. The distinction is sometimes rather difficult to follow since, in a truly absolute monarchy such as this, the government and the monarch cannot be separated: there were no institutions, and are none today, to interpose between the king and the government, which are, in fact, one. After all, when Louis XIV declared 'I am the State', he declared it to the Parlement of Paris, an ancient legal body which antedated both him and his family; but there is no such body in Arabia. The wondrous wealth which descended upon Abd el-Aziz in his declining years seemed to him—by most of the available evidence—personal, and with all such goods it was his first instinct to be as generous as possible. He could not give it all away but he tried, and his natural benevolence exceeded the limits hitherto known. What he created, in the way of institutions and traditions, was more or less the work of instinct or the unconscious: he was that phenomenon not at all unknown in history, a genius creating something of which he knew almost nothing.

And yet within his own family there was an element of comprehension which surpassed his own. That was the mind of his third son, Faisal. The eldest, Turki, had died, and the Crown Prince during the last years of the old King's life was Sa'ud, a handsome and amiable man who had no real comprehension, it would seem, of history or government. The third was Faisal, who is now king.

The oil men had their troubles with the old King but always found that he was instinctively understanding. He respected them, without in the least fearing them—on the contrary, they feared him: he could have tossed them out at any moment. But he did not truly know what they were doing and he never learned, nor did he pretend to do so. He looked at those vast establishments just as I do and said 'What hath God wrought!' They got along very well. His successor, King Sa'ud, a great spender and builder, who brought the treasury of the kingdom to exhaustion in eleven years, was always at them for an advance of five million dollars or so (or three or ten) and although such sums are small in comparison to the annual income, I have been solemnly assured that Aramco never gave King Sa'ud so much as a single million which had not already been earned—in other words, they paid him what they would have had to pay him anyhow a little later under the royalty agreements. This is in contrast to stories I have heard from Arab sources to the effect that he owed the company $300,000,000 at one time, which to me would seem quite a little advance. I think all such stories have been exaggerated, but in the frenzied finance of the late 1950's it is certainly quite possible (as some of my friends insist) that King Sa'ud's borrowings, although not from Aramco itself, did mortgage his future very heavily.

However that may be, Sa'ud certainly went to the Aramco concessions in the Eastern Province more often that his father and took more interest in them. It was there, at his palace near Damman, that I saw him in 1960 and liked him very much, although without much confidence in his intellect. His younger brother Faisal, then Crown Prince and Prime Minister, had arranged this. I cannot forget the deferential way in which King Sa'ud referred to his brother. 'My brother says . . .' was the introduction to a polite sentence of welcome. Actually there was small opportunity for conversation. He sat on a throne at one end of the room and a very large number of desert sheikhs as well as notables from the Eastern Province came to kneel before him and kiss his hand. I sat beside him on a small chair and admired the Persian carpets which had been arrayed on the walls and floor. We were about a hundred and eighty or two hundred at dinner, all grim males with beards, and afterwards when the water was poured over His Majesty's hands, which was the signal for my departure, he invited me to put my fingers also under the water over the golden bowl.

In the garden, which had been strewn with very grand Persian carpets, where we sat for quite a while before this, there was a powerful odour of petroleum.

3   The Wahhabi Movement

1

STRANGE it seems to reflect now that when I first went to Riyadh, the royal and ancestral capital of the Sa'udi dynasty, I was warned against smoking cigarettes in public or otherwise offending the prejudices of the population.

That was only in 1960, and yet in this short period a world has changed. Foreigners go everywhere in Riyadh today, and not only do they smoke cigarettes at will but a great many of the inhabitants do the same. The change has been quite visible through these years. There were few foreigners there in 1960—the American military mission for instruction in automatic weapons was scarcely to be seen, and although I inhabited the same hotel as they, I never beheld them— and possibly the anxious admonitions given me by the Swiss hotel manager were reasonable and necessary. Riyadh was just coming out of a long isolation which had made it in some respects almost as impermeable as Lhasa in Tibet. In the days of the old King (who died only in 1953, we must remember) it was advisable for any foreigner visiting the capital to dress in Arab clothing. This was not any idea of disguise, of course, which would have been useless, but as a tribute to the customs of the country.

As a guest of the Crown Prince and Prime Minister (who now is King) I was probably watched over anyhow, although I never noticed any form of surveillance. But I do remember with amusement the anxiety of the Swiss hotel manager, who felt himself personally involved, in some way personally responsible to the Crown Prince for my safety, and therefore frightened at my western carelessness, not to say recklessness, in the face of a whole system of ideas and code of conduct alien to me.

His perturbation was unnecessary because I had known of the Wahhabi movement and the Wahhabi scale of values for more than forty years. As a junior in the University of Chicago (1920) I had studied under Professor Ferdinand Schevill (formerly Schwill I think) in a course on the fall of the Ottoman Empire in which this movement in the desert had been an element of high interest to me; I had written my final study ('term-paper' it was called) on that subject. The idea of the desert puritanism had never left me, and it was partly in a continuation of such an interest, along with others which had arisen during the long interval, that I was now in Arabia.

So, I smoked few cigarettes in public, strolled sedately in frequented streets and made myself as inconspicuous as it is possible for such a very large western foreigner to be. I was conscious of being stared at a great deal, since, at that time, I was a rare bird in the place; it was only natural; since then all has changed in Riyadh. Foreigners are hardly noticed any more, and if I were only four inches shorter nobody would look at me in the street. I have been in Riyadh five times since then, the latest only a few months ago, and I doubt if I have attracted any attention, but in 1960 I was like a two-headed elephant.

These observations over a short segment of 'elapsed' time (the airman's word) lead to a conclusion, I think, which it is hardly possible to refute. It is that fanaticism fades, xenophobia declines and puritanism weakens in the face of ordinary human experience. Those interested in Arabia (I cannot speak for a larger world) must have known for at least one century or one and a half, in a general way, about the Wahhabi movement, and have thought of it as being puritanical, fanatical and fiercely opposed to all foreigners. This is what the books of reference have said, and what the travellers (so few!) have reported. As a child in Illinois I learned it. In 1960, and on recurrent occasions since then, I have run into anything but these disagreeable characteristics. I find openness, hospitality and candour; I find no hostility of any kind, except in argument (which is a healthy symptom in any country); I have yet to discover a Nejdi Arab, that is, a devout follower of the so-called Wahhabi fanaticism, who regards me as an enemy. If there had been such, I should have known it, because there are things well understood through the clouds of language, culture and manners.

2

Sheikh Mohammed ibn Abd el-Wahhab was born in 1691, according to most authorities, and died in 1787. During his very long life he had the experience which philosophers, teachers and preachers have always wanted: he found a man of action to put his ideas into practice.

He was an idealist, a reformer, a fiery preacher for what he thought right. It may be that it was more suited to the central and eastern deserts of Arabia than to any other place or condition of mankind. Unlike the Prophet Mohammed, he had no tenderness for his enemies, for the disbelievers, for the Jews and the Christians (whom he abominated) or for any Muslims who disagreed with him. The resemblance to what Christians call 'puritans' and to 'puritanism' cannot be put aside: it is there, in the entire literature of the subject, because we cannot think of Abd el-Wahhab without thinking of similar impulses or movements elsewhere. Like John Knox in Scotland or Calvin in Switzerland three centuries earlier, the Sheikh Mohammed actually put virtue into sumptuary regulations, as if you could achieve paradise by refusing to wear silk. This psychological state is what we call 'puritanism' in the west, and no matter what qualifications may be made for place or time, it is still perfectly recognizable.

It includes, of course (as in the west), a stern condemnation of those shadowy idolatries which lead to the worship of saints, local deities and natural phenomena. Monotheism is supreme, as always in Islam (and as the Sheikh Mohammed feared it might not always be). There had been a tremendous degeneration into humbler forms of prayer for intercession, just as there was in Christianity. (We all know the Italian peasant who, having lost her best milk crock by some natural calamity such as breaking on a stone, prays to St. Antony of Padua to restore it.) The Sheikh Mohammed made a crashing attack upon such superstitions and weaknesses—he called them 'abominations'—and it was because, through them, he saw a way into idolatry, a relapse into what had once debased the Arabs. Perhaps he was right in so thinking —there is evidence of idolatrous practises—but right or wrong, he prevailed.

He prevailed, as we shall see, through his connection with the House of Sa'ud and its devotion to his principles.

At the same time there was something of far wider import to Islam in Abd el-Wahhab's teaching than could be limited by Nejd or any such region of Arabia. It caught on rather quickly in the eighteenth century because of the conditions of the central desert and the threat of the Turkish power. The Turks were rich, luxurious and corrupt— so much could be seen—and their pretence of being Muslim was not utterly convincing to an Arab. They could not speak Arabic and generally hated the Arabs. The Bedouin of the central and eastern deserts had so far been spared their depredations, but not their shadow, and it was clear to all in the desert that they were the enemy. Indeed the Jews and the Christians, although known in language and camp-fire stories, did not actually exist in the country, as they do not today. Whom, then, is the Bedu of the central desert to hate? Obviously he must hate the possessors, those who have everything he has not, and if he can feel quite sure that they are morally and psychologically corrupt, guilty in possessing that which they possess, wicked in enjoying that which they enjoy, then he must destroy them.

I may have expressed this crudely enough, and yet there is some-thing of the kind in every militant puritanism known to us. The faith, in such conditions and when life is otherwise hard and limited, implies a vigorous hatred for those who have either wandered away from it or do not share it. The history of Christianity provides examples enough.

The Sheikh found his audience in the desert and town dwellers of the centre and southeast, and in emphasising his message he seems to have passed over the gentler and more benevolent parts of the Islamic mission. He seems not to acknowledge the warrior's reward (even such as were promised in Paradise) but only his obligation. Un-doubtedly he felt that his emphasis was needed if Islam (so far as he could reach it) was to return to the true faith.

Intrepid, learned and eloquent though he was, his austere version of the religion might not have flourished as it did for at least a century and a half if he had not obtained a devoted follower in the great Mohammed ibn Sa'ud, Sheikh or Emir of Nejd. This man, a thinker and doer who had no fear, accepted the teacher, the like of whom he had probably never beheld, undoubtedly because he was convinced, a true believer, as were his descendants to be.

And when the House of Sa'ud accepted this stern mission it was with the full realization that it would probably mean, on the actual stage of human events, war after war. For the way the desert princes saw their duty, it was to compel by fire and sword that which they firmly believed. Only through the teachings of the Sheikh could a man become a true Muslim. That was the way the doctrine worked itself out in actual life.

39

The Sa'udi family originated in Dari'yah, below what is now Riyadh in the central-eastern realm of Nejd. The buildings that once were there have been almost engulfed by the sand, which, once you leave the main motor-road, makes travel by Cadillac something of a problem. I have visited it twice, and with the same results. Small boys come laughing from nowhere to extricate the fat tyres of the American motor-car from the conquering sand. You can climb to the ruins of Dari'yah, if you wish, and see really nothing beyond a few mud walls and brown slopes. The oasis has at least one important spring but although its wheezy pump seems incessant the results do not appear. It does seem a small origin for a great result.

Mohammed ibn Sa'ud, who reigned from 1747 to 1765 at Dari'yah, was the son of the eponymous chief, Sa'ud the Great, upon whom the entire dynasty was based. Of course there were innumberable ancestors, reaching through many generations in Arab history and in legend as far back as Abraham, as is the case with most Arab royal families. Even so, Sa'ud the Great and his son Mohammed, whom I might call the Greater, were not tremendous overlords in the tribal world. Their tribes, herds and water-holes, territories for roaming and occasions for plunder, were originally small. Their instincts and their eventual faith enabled them to overwhelm those who could not overwhelm them. It was the social and economic system of the desert.

The Sheikh Mohammed Abd el-Wahhab, beyond doubt a man of genius, persuaded these semi-nomads and nomads that they had a cause, which was the redemption of Islam. He told them mono-theism was in danger because under the influence of the Turks (hardly better than Jews and Christians) there had been shrines erected in the peninsula. Such shrines were dedicated to various powerful spirits of good and evil, some of the most respectable being Mother Eve, Father Adam and Father Abraham. The veneration and almost worship of such patrons is widespread in the Arab world.

The Sheikh and the valiant warrior who upheld him, Mohammed ibn Sa'ud, were both great men, and hardly anything in modern Arab history can compare to their achievement. Is it not clear and certain that their memory has animated all of their descendants? Is it not inevitable that the thought of them must dwell in the mind of the present King, Faisal of Sa'udi Arabia, even if only in the subregions of the consciousness, though he has travelled so far and seen so much? Faisal is descended from Mohammed ibn Sa'ud collaterally by his brother Abdullah, and he is descended also quite directly from the Sheikh himself, whom we call (we westerners) Abd el-Wahhab. The

King's mother was a great-granddaughter in (I think) the eighth generation from the great Sheikh. The King's grandfather (his mother's father) was also a Muslim divine of immense authority, also called Sheikh Mohammed Abd el-Wahhab, and it was in his house that the young Faisal spent his childhood and youth.

These things certainly must have their effect upon any growing mind, no matter how far off the ancestors may be. I have found no sign of fanaticism in King Faisal today, and indeed we have heard him give tongue to some astonishing expressions of ecumenism, such as his declaration in Khartoum (March, 1966, when I accompanied him and many others on a state visit) that 'all the great monotheisms' should work together against subversion and atheism. By 'all the great monotheisms' he must mean chiefly the Jews and the Christians, because they are the only other strict, concrete montheisms we know on the world scale. It may be argued that both Hinduism and Buddhism are essentially monotheistic, the latter in objective fact (obscured by mysticisms of all sorts) and the former under the guise of polytheistic representations (the goddess of learning being merely an *aspect* of the One God). This, however, is hair-splitting: to a western mind the three great monotheisms are those Faisal meant—Islam, Christianity and Judaism. His great-great-great-granduncle Mohammed ibn-Sa'ud, the warrior friend and adherent of Abd el-Wahhab, as well as that firebrand himself, would have been astonished to hear the infidel so accepted.

From the time Mohammed ibn-Sa'ud adopted the stern and uncompromising creed of Sheikh Mohammed Abd el-Wahhab there was war in the central desert—war for the faith, for the new faith whose adherents insisted that it was simply the old faith revived and reinforced. The combination of a vigorous warrior prince and a religious movement of deep psychological power has always been dynamic in its course and results: and so it was here. Perhaps the combination has a stronger magic in the desert because war and religion were very nearly the only public interest the Bedouin possessed: in the absence of commerce and industry, social and economic effort or any form of political deliberation, what else could there be? The Wahhabi prince and his religious mentor conquered region after region, all in and around Nejd, in this sudden spurt of the ancestral activity. After Mohammed's death his son Abd el-Aziz, who reigned from 1765 to 1803, spread the conquests out in all directions, even to the west and south, including the capture of Mecca itself.

The appeal of the Wahhabi faith as such—as distinct from the effectiveness of its armed force—does not seem to have worked at all outside the central desert. Puritanism or asceticism could not exert much influence upon Arabs who had been in contact with the world at large for centuries, as was the case on the Red Sea coast; the inhabitants of Mecca and Medina endured the Wahhabi conquest but did not accept the Wahhabi view of life. They had their own ways of eating, dressing, working, praying; much of what the Wahhabi had to say was expressed in uncouth Bedouin dialect which the coast-dwellers could scarcely understand; the general sharpness and bitterness of the doctrine made it inharmonious to the character of the Hedjaz folk, who, from the standpoint of a superior culture, could afford to live through the experience and ignore its content.

Here I speak of specific 'conversion', i.e. of the acceptance of Wahhabi doctrine voluntarily by persons who had not professed it before and had perhaps not even known of it except by the vaguest hearsay. This we do not meet and I have read of no such experiences. The Wahhabi probably made no effort to make converts; their contempt for their fellow-Arabs in cities and civilized countries was so strong that they would have disdained to try. And there was a notable obstacle, that is, the comfortable habit of life, in the way of any city Arab who suddenly felt drawn to the Bedouin life and its stern faith. For these and for no doubt many other reasons the Wahhabi movement, which in its earlier phases was remarkably like the beginnings of Islam itself, lost that resemblance at contact with the outside world and, instead of flowering, fell upon decay.

Professor Bayly Winder has pointed out (*Saudi Arabia in the Nineteenth Century*) that the influence of the movement was nevertheless profound in the Muslim thinking of the last century, spreading even after the movement itself had been turned back to its desert—spreading, no doubt, in part because the political and military danger had been removed. He quotes Professor H. A. R. Gibb (*Modern Trends in Islam*) as saying:

> But in its ideal aspect, in the challenge which it flung out to the contamination of pure Islamic monotheism by the infiltration of animistic practises and pantheistic notions, Wahhabism had a salutary and revitalizing effect, which spread little by little over the whole Muslim world.

That is, of course, the Muslim *intellectual* world: it would be hard to imagine the masses in Damascus, Baghdad or Cairo devoting much attention to a puritanical reform movement in the central desert of

Arabia. In the universities and among the theoretical writers there was a stirring, just the same, even if it was only curiosity in disguise: it had in fact been quite some time since an original Arab–Islamic statement had been made with the backing of some kind of force and organization. The Wahhabi rigidity in theology, which saw dreadful invasions of polytheism in many practices of modern Islam, was accompanied by an equal rigidity in the interpretation of ethical precepts in the Koran and in the traditions of the Prophet's Companions. In the first instance, the theology of the One God, a great deal of ritual and ceremonial had grown up about tombs and domes and memorials; all of this was idolatry in the Wahhabite's eyes, and the remedy was death and destruction. Thus a raiding party of Bedouin, faithful Wahhabi, crossed into Iraq in 1801 and destroyed or damaged the tombs at Kerbela, the holiest place to the Shia branch of Islam. Some years later the tomb of Mother Eve on the Red Sea coast fared no better, when the Bedouin hordes took Mecca. As for the interpretation of the Koran and the traditions, Wahhabi doctrine held that nothing after the third century A.H. (roughly 900 A.D.) could be acceptable as orthodox.

In this case a return to the old was equivalent, as so often, to the discovery of the new, and it is quite certain that when it was at its lowest ebb politically (during the Egyptian occupation in 1818–1822 and the decades just following) the Wahhabi doctrine was freshening the minds and enlivening the talk of young men from Baghdad to Cairo.

3

The dynasty of Sa'ud was indissolubly connected with the Wahhabi doctrine in the minds of all Arabs. The difference was that the secular dynasty was subject to secular pressures and could disappear altogether for some years, as it did twice in the past century. The religion could not disappear from those regions where it had taken root in the hearts of the people. And, as might have been foreseen, the religion served as a mighty weapon when the Sa'ud family was able to begin the work of restoration: it always gave members of that clan an advantage over all rivals because they were the warriors of Abd el-Wahhab himself, and were by this time his relatives and descendants as well. (Inter-marriages between the House of Sa'ud and the descendants of Abd el-Wahhab became frequent.) As Ibn Khaldun (as quoted by Professor Winder) once said, nomads plus religion equal power—rather an Americanized statement for an Arab scholar of the thirteenth century.

What is obvious is that the combination of the will to power and the will to preach made the Sa'ud-Wahhab partnership unique in desert politics of modern times, so that it could not be defeated for long, and in spite of conditions approaching chaos, with dozens of tribal chieftains contesting every material prize, it came eventually to supremacy over all Arabia.

The way was long and hard. Mohammed ibn-Sa'ud's son, Abd el-Aziz (1765–1803) brought the Sa'udi empire to an early pitch of glory by extending the directly governed territories from Shammar to Oman and from Qatar to the Hedjaz, with the grand prize of Mecca not far off. The indirectly governed territories, or those which merely paid tribute and recognized a suzerainty, were scattered around the edges of this Wahhabi nucleus. Whole tribes in the province of Asir (above Yemen on the Red Sea) declared themselves to be Wahhabi, and the same thing happened to whole tribes in the hinterland of Oman, at the other side of the peninsula. In fact such 'conversions', being of a political nature, did not survive the success which they celebrated, and there are few in those regions who would today declare themselves Wahhabi in doctrine or practice.

Abd el-Aziz Ibn Mohammed was murdered at Dar'iyah, the ancestral capital, in 1803, by a devout Shia who was avenging the Bedouin raid at Kerbela two years before. His eldest son Sa'ud succeeded, reigning successfully from 1803 to 1814, and the capture of Mecca (1806) was only the high point of an expansive, prosperous epoch. The Wahhabi behaved none too well in their first appearance on the Red Sea coast, and the dread of their bloodthirsty puritanism remained in the air for a long time afterwards.

The control of the Holy Cities by heretics, as Muslims in general considered the Wahhabi to be, was not to be tolerated by the Sublime Porte in Constantinople. The Sultans of the Ottoman Turks had called themselves 'servants of the holy cities' or of the 'holy places' or 'shrines' (el-Haramain el-Sharifain) since the sixteenth century, and had exerted some effort at maintaining order since then. For them to be expelled from this office, which was the foundation of their claim to the caliphate, could not be endured for long, as the Wahhabi would have known if they had known more of the world. What they incurred from the Turks was no less than their own destruction, at least for a time, and grievous sufferings for their people.

The Sublime Porte itself was enfeebled by many preoccupations, but its viceroy in Egypt, Mohammed Ali the Albanian, was flushed with success and ready for further tasks. The Sultan named him commander for an Arabian expedition and governor after he got there. Mohammed Ali himself assumed the charge at first, and during 1812–1813 he prosecuted the war with vigour, capturing the Holy Cities and putting them again under Ottoman rule. It seemed even then that the war would be long, since the Egyptian forces, although trained and equipped in western style, had no decisive superiority over the Bedouin. They won but never decisively enough to sweep an entire province clear or break the Wahhabi opposition. Thus it took seven long years for them to reach Dar'iyah, the Bedu capital, and seven months longer for them to besiege the mud city and force its surrender. By this time the commander and governor was no longer Mohammed Ali, but his son Ibrahim, who had taken over some years before, displaying that hardened cruelty which distinguished him even in a semi-barbarous culture. The Sa'udi sovereign of Nejd was Abdullah, son of Sa'ud, son of Abd el-Aziz, son of Mohammed ibn-Sa'ud the first Wahhabi ruler. Ibrahim made some conditions with Abdullah but none were kept. The Sa'udi king was sent off to Constantinople where, eventually, he was beheaded; the massacre of his followers was notable even for the Turks; his capital, Dar'yah, was reduced to a rubbish-heap.

One of Ibrahim's economies deserves attention. He found that sending the heads of his victims to Cairo was long, slow and expensive. He therefore compromised: after the execution of prisoners, by sending their ears only to his august father in Cairo he could get credit for just as many Wahhabi heads, although at much less cost.

The famine and desolation which swept over Arabia at this period were shared by the Egyptians, since they had no other supplies than those levied from the inhabitants. They are said to have eaten grass at times—although grass is about as rare as grain or dates in Arabia, generally more so.

They were uncomfortable at Nejd and in the eastern parts of the peninsula in general; only the Hedjaz seemed hospitable to them; they felt the almost universal hostility of the Arab population even when it had not flamed into violence. Thus it was no surprise when they were ordered (from Cairo, by Mohammed Ali) to evacuate the whole country with the exception of the Hedjaz, but to see that the Wahhabi were wiped out before doing so.

All important members of the House of Sa'ud had to be sent as prisoners to Cairo, the mosques, houses and villages of that family must be destroyed, every fortified place in the Bedouin tracts must be razed to the ground, and so far as was humanly possible it must be ensured that Egypt would never have to worry about the Wahhabi Bedouin again.

All this was done, and more, with the result that Nejd suffered a more completely 'Carthaginian' peace than Europe or the Middle East had known for centuries. Having reduced it to chaos, the Turks ignored it thereafter, and the entire area became the prey of raider and counter-raider in a tangle of violence which seemed to increase as there grew progressively less to loot.

There were, even so, stirrings among the ruins. There were chiefs of importance who could claim tribal following, and there were even remnants of the House of Sa'ud left, including one Mushari (brother of the last ruler) who succeeded in escaping from his guards on the way to Egypt. Mushari made a brief restoration of Sa'udi rule in Nejd, only to provoke a renewal of the Egyptian occupation, worse than before. In these topsy-turvy conditions, where there was no central authority and little of any kind, Turki, a grandson of Mohammed ibn Sa'ud by the younger son Abdullah, was gradually assuming the position of leadership in the Sa'udi clans and briefly set up his capital at Riyadh in 1819–1820, only to be driven out again by the renewed Turkish occupation.

There was by now a difference, however, in that Turki ibn Abdullah ibn Mohammed was now the only Sa'udi prince left alive and free in Arabia—the others had all been killed or carried off to exile. Turki had escaped by a narrow margin, having left Riyadh and gone into hiding only a few hours before the arrival of the Turks. He was probably concealed amongst the southern tribes, in the inaccessible 'Empty Quarter', from 1820 to 1823, but in that year he reappeared in central Arabia with an appeal for aid against the Turks, and found that many Bedouin were ready to follow him. His main action had to be a siege of Riyadh, which, after months, was forced to surrender. (He gave the garrison *aman*, that is, permission to go in peace, provided they left Nejd; and he kept his word, unlike Ibrahim.) This was followed by a rapid series of successes of the same kind, so that by 1825 Turki ruled Nejd again as Imam, as his ancestors had done before him. He did not have the whole of Nejd—significantly, the Jebel Shammar region was outside his realm and would soon become a plague to the House of Sa'ud; both east and west the new imamate was circumscribed more than its predecessors.

Moreover, there may have been some limitation on absolute

independence—that is, Turki may have paid some tribute, or in some other way acknowledged suzerainty of the Turk. Whatever it was, the Turks allowed him to rule in peace and he was able to consolidate his regime by vanquishing a number of Bedu tribes and collecting their back taxes.

During this period there were Bedouin raids on the Hedjaz, and more or less in all other directions outside the state of Nejd, but how much Sa'udi responsibility can be assigned for these expeditions is uncertain. The family of el-Rashid, hereditary overlords of Jebel Shammar, were dispossessed during the Egyptian chaos and made friends of Turki, visiting Riyadh and submitting to his authority. Thus the groundwork was laid for large claims covering most of Arabia, although in reality the realm of Turki was only the hard core of Nejd, and Wahhabi at that.

Turki's triumphs culminated in 1830 with the quick conquest of the great Hasa oasis and the adjacent territories which today together form the Eastern Province. This included, for a while, even the islands of Bahrein, which soon afterwards (1833) slipped out of control again and remained independent thereafter.

These and other achievements may have rejoiced the ruler of Riyadh, but he must have taken special pleasure in another event of the period, which was the escape of his son and heir, Faisal, from his guards in Egypt and his subsequent return to Arabia and to Nejd (1828 probably). When Turki was assassinated on coming from midday prayer at the mosque in Riyadh (May 9th, 1834) Faisal was at Hufuf in the Eastern Province, but it took him no more than a month to organize his forces, march across the desert and annihilate the makeshift government of the assassins. His reign began auspiciously; he even forgave all his enemies, the rebels, except those actually involved in the murder of his father; his authority was acknowledged in all the provinces and even (in Oman and Hedjaz) a little beyond.

Mohammed Ali, who had now revolted against the Sublime Porte and by means of war aspired to an independent Egypt, was much irked by the rise of a new Wahhabi power from the ashes which he had thought permanent. He equipped a new expedition under Ismail Bey to relieve the much-harassed Ahmad Pasha in Mecca and to press against the Wahhabi wherever possible. For this a perfect political instrument was at hand—the boy Khalid, youngest son of Sa'ud and therefore brother of the last Imam of that line. Ismail's army entered Arabia with Khalid in its train and the memories of Egyptian outrages were still so vivid in the country that many hastened to join him. The way was cleared for a brief reign for Khalid, who, how-ever, was too obviously a puppet of the Turks (Egyptians) to suit most of the Wahhabi. Having been brought up in Cairo under the eye of Mohammed Ali, this young prince was Europeanized to a degree and could scarcely be considered Wahhabi at all, in spite of his ancestry. Faisal, at Hufuf in the Eastern Province, kept his forces intact during this period and waited until a serious Egyptian defeat at Hilway encouraged him to another siege of Riyadh. This failed too; there was a sort of checkmate between Khalid and Faisal, who exercised the sovereignty between them for a while on a very rough partition basis. In the course of the confused fighting the new Turkish (Egyptian) commander, Khurshid Pasha, captured Faisal in battle and sent the Imam off to Cairo a second time as prisoner (December, 1838).

During this entire period the ambition of Mohammed Ali and his son Ibrahim had aimed at nothing less than an empire to be carved out of the moribund body of the Ottoman realm. Palestine, Syria and Arabia itself (with the Hedjaz as firm nucleus) were parts of the great plan formed by these Albanian *condottieri*, with Egypt as their base and source of supply. The plans went extraordinarily well for a while, chiefly because of the corruption and incompetence of the Turkish forces, while Mohammed Ali's troops were mainly Arab and under westernized discipline. In such a hotch-potch of races and regional origins it is impossible to talk of 'nationality', and yet it was cus-tomary, by the end of the 1830's, to call Mohammed Ali's very mixed forces 'Egyptians'. They were mainly Arabs commanded by Turks, Albanians, Georgians and others who were traitors to the Ottoman Sultan. The break-up of Turkey, one of the nightmares of European diplomacy during the nineteenth century—not that Turkey was a good thing but that the diplomats feared what might come after-wards—now seemed to be, again as so often later, about to occur.

There followed an intervention of the great powers, with only France (the France of Louis-Philippe) to uphold Mohammed Ali's claims. Under the united pressure of Europe it was impossible for the Albanian adventurer to persist, and he was forced to retire upon his base—to be content with Egypt, which, considering that he started with nothing, was indeed quite a prize.

The fortunes of Nejd were determined, at this period, by events and circumstances afar off, of which the desert Arabs knew nothing. Palmerston in England, Nesselrode in Russia, Metternich in Austria, Louis-Philippe in France, were arbiters of destiny during the 1830's, and none of them (except France) could contemplate the disintegration of the Ottoman Empire without anxiety. Thus they came together in an agreement (1840) to clip Mohammed Ali's wings, and as a result the Egyptians were obliged to withdraw from all Arabia except the Holy Cities. Khalid ibn-Sa'ud, the puppet prince through whom Egypt had ruled Nejd for two years, was now left alone and his unpopularity became evident; a cousin, Ibn Thunaiyan, dethroned him and reigned for a few confused months; then the Imam Faisal, who had been a prisoner in Egypt for five years, made a dashing escape from his jailers and returned to Arabia (1843) to be rapidly acknowledged as sovereign by tribes and townsmen alike.

Thus began the longest of the Sa'udi reigns up to this century. Philby says in his *Arabia*:

Faisal now entered upon an unchallenged reign of all but a quarter of a century, in which must be sought the real beginnings of the modern Wahhabi state. . . . [He] ruled a territory considerably smaller in extent than that of his great ancestors, but perhaps more compact and better woven together on the loom of Wahhabism. A new generation had grown up whose oldest members knew not the Jacob of the old paganism, whose faded and perished remnants may yet be found in our day as patches on the new garment of dour dogmatism which passes for philosophy among the nomad tribes of the desert. The Arabia of Faisal was Wahhabi, in a sense unknown to the heyday of the Wahhabi empire; and Faisal's reign was one of administrative consolidation and progress in education and other acts of peace, leading up, by the irony of fate, to a final tragedy of dynastic dissension.

Faisal was able, skilled, moderate in language and negotiation; he was a pious Wahhabi and his days were dotted with prayers and scriptural readings; no sooner was he firmly established in his sovereignty at Riyadh than he made Abd el-Latif, a grandson of 'the Sheikh' (as Abd el-Wahhab is called among Wahhabi), his court chaplain. He was well received by all the tribes except, after a while, the Unaizah of Qasim, and the tribal dissensions set up in that province plagued the greater part of his life. On the other hand, he maintained the friendliest relations with two or three generations of the family of Ibn Rashid, supreme in the Jebel Shammar, who never failed to support him in war and acknowledge his sovereignty. One of the Rashidi (Ubaid, brother of the chief of the clan) spent several months a year with Faisal in Riyadh. It would have been difficult to foresee, in the best period of Faisal's reign, that the Rashidi would turn out to be the bitterest enemies of the Sa'udi and for a time their merciless, victorious rivals.

Around the edges of the diminished empire it was not so easy to govern or even to obtain the tributes in money, animals or goods which had been customary. Qasim was always turbulent; to the east and south (the Persian Gulf and Oman) there were constant troubles. The tiny states which together are called the 'Trucial States' (because they signed the 'Perpetual Truce' with Great Britain) were more and more creeping under the British wing, and Bahrein, to which the Wahhabi made claim as suzerains, was ever rebellious. In 1861 when a new treaty or truce was made in the region Bahrein, too, descended to the level of a British protectorate, in which status it was to remain (and grow rich!). In general it may be said that the British influence or even power, based upon a naval squadron, grew constantly stronger in the whole Persian Gulf reign. The British goals were clearly defined and were repeated in a number of documents of the period: they were to suppress piracy, keep the Gulf clear for trade, and maintain peace on the water. Inland Arabia, according to many declarations which were in fact maintained, did not concern Great Britain.

Faisal as Imam (1843–1865) was stern and extremely devout, but by no means cruel—in fact his generosity to many treacherous tribal chiefs became proverbial in Arabia. He suffered the loss of considerable territory and territorial claims but perhaps, as Philby suggests, derived the advantage of a more compact, homogeneous realm than that of Sa'ud the Great. In his last years, enfeebled and totally blind, he was obliged to rely more and more upon his sons, and chiefly upon his eldest son Abdullah, who proved himself capable as a field commander and governor. At his death in December, 1865 (according to some reports, it was of a cholera epidemic from India), he was succeeded by this son as Amir of Nejd and Imam of the Wahhabi.

Faisal had four sons. These were the able, hard-headed, experienced Abdullah (whom Philby calls 'dull-witted'), and his brother Sa'ud, Mohammed and Abd el-Rahman. The third son, Mohammed, supported his elder, but the second son, Sa'ud, who had been acting as a semi-independent governor in the southern area of Nejd (Kharj and thereabouts) was the prey of great jealousy and hatred. This hatred between Abdullah and Sa'ud was to prove the downfall of the House of Sa'ud once again, and ruin of the final, irremediable kind seemed to have descended upon it before the century's end.

Of Faisal's four sons all but the third, Mohammed, had himself proclaimed Imam at some time or other, and after Sa'ud's death from smallpox (1875) his own four sons set up their claims to the throne. All of this was accomplished by bloodshed on a greater or lesser scale —sometimes there was a sort of platonic warfare in which the menace took the place of the deed; sometimes (as in the final stages) there was butchery. And, as always in the wars of Arabia, the stronger force carried away camels and cut down date-palms, the two sources of desert well-being. The sufferings of the people mounted; there are horrendous descriptions of what they were forced to eat (the corpses of dead donkeys, for instance) and of their consequent diseases and death. So far as one can tell from the evidence, there was never any reason for this except the insane ambition of Sa'ud ibn Faisal, who, although his elder brother had long been fully recognized as heir to the throne, and was in fact well suited to his duties, nevertheless could not resign himself to taking second place.

Meanwhile, of course, the Sa'udi dominions were falling apart and the rival House of Rashid in Jebel Shammar was growing strong. There had been dynastic rivalries in that family, too, but Mohammed ibn Rashid emerged as the strong man at this time and, patient as well as strong, held his hand while the Sa'udi brothers destroyed each other. At one point Abdullah, having been ousted by Sa'ud, called upon the Turks to come to his aid; they were delighted to do so, occupied the Eastern Province, and did not leave it again until the war of 1914 pushed them out. Abdullah was Imam three different times, with Sa'ud reigning between; then the sons of Sa'ud set up highly impermanent regimes when they could. To 'restore order', and at the request of Abdullah himself against his nephews, Mohammed ibn Rashid descended upon Riyadh as conqueror at the end of 1887 and carried the Imam Abdullah off with him to Hail. The Wahhabi state had now perished and what remained of it territorially (only the central districts of Nejd) was ruled by the Rashidi thereafter, up to the coming of the Great King.

Abd el-Rahman, the youngest son of Faisal, made some slight attempt at revolt but it was useless. He took his way into exile at Kuwait, where the ruler gave him asylum—to him and to his young son Abd el-Aziz, then ten years of age. They must have arrived in Kuwait, after wandering in disguise in the desert and hiding in the towns, along about April, 1891.

4 King Abd El-Aziz

1

THE exile to which Abd el-Rahman went in Kuwait was not an easy one. The ruler of Kuwait, Mohammed ibn Sabah, although by no means as rich as his descendants have become, was possessed of enough resources to be generous if he had wished. He had an old friendship for the House of Sa'ud, he had no reason to favour the House of Rashid, which was indeed coming much too close to his own small realm; and he was bound, like all Arabs, to give asylum to a fugitive, hospitality to a guest. Nevertheless he was niggardly and, above all, afraid. He was sitting at the head of the Persian Gulf in an extremely strategic position, fending off year after year the favours and protection of those who might have taken over his principality: the Turks—whose suzerainty was vague—and the British, whose naval squadron effectively controlled the Gulf and kept its ports open. Long before the discovery of its fabulous petroleum deposits Kuwait had been the envy of the neighbours for its port and its advantageous geography; even Mohammed Ali had coveted it, from Cairo, and it was mainly by an astute balancing of one 'friend' against another that the Sheikh of Kuwait was able to maintain himself in relative security and independence. His port was the chief one for camels, dates and pearls: from Kuwait to Bahrein to Muscat at the other end of the Gulf there was nothing of comparable importance.

The exiles from Nejd were, like all exiles, embarrassing to their host at times. There were intervals when it suited the policy of the principality to keep them out of sight, and at other times it was more useful to push them forward, depending upon who had to be cajoled, intimidated or deceived. The humiliation of such a situation were deeply perceived by Abd el-Rahman and even his young son Abd el-Aziz, who was already dreaming (or so the stories have it in Arabia) of a return to Nejd.

In his later years King Abd el-Aziz was a great story-teller (as most Arabs are) and loved to sit on the roof of his palace at night, munching his favourite supper of fruit, telling tales of the old days. I have had accounts of this from many persons, some of them quite young when the old King died, but who for various reasons went to that hospitable repast under the moon. One of these was Sheikh Abd el-Aziz Majid, now the chief interpreter for King Faisal, who was then just beginning in court office. They all tell me that reminiscence was the substance of the King's discourse, and many of his stories (such as the one about the capture of Riyadh) had been told so many times that they did not vary a word or an iota: they had been crystallized by memory and the natural sense of drama, gesture, inflection and emphasis which is deep in all Arabs.

Even so, although many heard the King's stories through the decades, the chances are that nobody heard them more often or more attentively than H. St. John Philby, the strange Englishman who devoted his life to the King and to Arabia. Among his many books on the subject there is one, *Arabian Jubilee* (1953), written during the King's lifetime but published in the year of his death, which gives some account of how the Wahhabi exiles lived in Kuwait, and it seems to me quite certain that this account was based on what the King told Philby, probably not once but many times, in the course of their very long friendship.

In his stately and leisured way, Philby summarizes the experience as follows:

. . . there, in the bosom of his family, the young 'Abd el-Aziz lived until the turn of the century. The stern tenets of the Wahhabi faith were the principal item of his educational curriculum, while his upbringing in secular matters was left to chance, and from the age of puberty onwards, to the privilege of attending the solemn coffee-parties of his elders and of listening to their often instructive and always entertaining conversation. He must in particular have derived much profit from regular attendance at the general audiences of his host, Sheikh Mubarak ibn Sabah, who was unquestionably one of the outstanding personalities of Arabia in those critical days, when German policy envisaged Kuwait as the terminus of the

Berlin–Baghdad railway. He must have been aware too at all times of the protecting shadow of the British Empire, felt rather than seen in the days before the Persian Gulf came to be regarded as a British lake: when the nebulous fiction of Ottoman sovereignty or suzerainty was scrupulously respected so long as it was not invoked in the interests of potentially hostile elements. It was undoubtedly at this period that the young 'Abd el-'Aziz developed a boyish admiration for British imperialism, which has accompanied him through life, modified only by the proviso that it should not impinge on his own sphere of activity. And it may well be that his brain began during these years to contemplate the possibility of building up an empire for himself out of the shattered fragments of his ancestors' dominions, now loosely held together by Muhammad ibn Rashid until his death in 1897. That event may well have been a decisive factor in his day-dreams, although it would be some years before he could be ready to give them substance.

Aside from these serious preoccupations, Philby tells us, the young prince had many diversions, more suited to his age: he rode horses and camels, went hunting with hawks and Saluqi (fleet desert hounds) and whiled away the evening hours over the campfire and the coffee, listening to the older men tell stories. The early marriage ('to keep one out of mischief') and the early bereavement were in Kuwait: that first bride, whom Abd el-Aziz mourned more or less all his life in spite of the large number of her successors. And throughout this period he had the constant companionship of his full-sister the Lady Nura, who was in fact the most lasting companion of his life. She was a year his elder; they were only six and seven, respectively, when their father was dethroned and carried off to Hail for the first time. They were eleven and ten when, after wanderings, the family found shelter in Kuwait: Philby has a wonderful little picture (less than a sentence) of the boy tucked into one saddle-bag on the camel's back while his sister was fitted into another on the other side—'as he well remembers to this day.'

Thus, in exile but also in relative freedom, the young prince came to his early maturity. We have heard from many sources (not Philby!) that his first youth was not altogether without some cloudy episodes, including Bedouin raids and other activities in the desert. Certainly he learned his desert fighting somewhere and somehow, unless we are to assume that he came to it by sheer instinct at the age of about twenty-one. The chances are that he raided with the Bedu both north

King Faisal bin Abd el-Aziz es Sa'ud, King of Saudi Arabia.

(above) *The Bedouin army of King Abd el-Aziz ibn Sa'ud on the march,
1911. This picture was taken by Captain William Shakespear, the first
European to meet the King.*

(below) *King Abd el-Aziz, King of Hejaz and Nejd, at an encampment in
the Hejaz after the capture of the province from the Sharif of Mecca in 1925.*

(above) *The Great Street of Riyadh, looking west from the East Gate. King Abd el-Aziz captured Riyadh from the Rashidis early in 1902 with a handful of men and established it once more as the Saudi capital. By making his first task the strengthening of the walls and recruiting tribes from the south to his cause, he ensured that the city remained his capital.*

(below) *The Great Mosque at Riyadh, the royal and ancestral capital of the Sa'udi dynasty and centre of the Wahhabi doctrine. Turki ibn Abdullah ibn Mohammed es-Sa'ud, Imam of Nejd, was assassinated at the mosque in 1834.*

(above) *Dari'yah—general view from the East Gate. This is the place where the Sa'ud family originated and was the home of Sa'ud the Great in the early eighteenth century. This photograph was taken by H. St. John Philby in 1917, the same year that he met King Abd el-Aziz.*

(below) *The market at Hofuf, capital of Hasa province and held by the Turks until captured by Abd el-Aziz in 1913. By this move, the province was once again returned to the Wahhabi empire and the Amir of Nejd renewed the family dominion over central Arabia.*

(above) *King Abd el-Aziz driving to Friday prayers in Jiddah shortly after its surrender to him in 1925. With the fall of this city the empire of the Sharif of Mecca collapsed, leaving the whole of the Hejaz in the hands of King Abd el-Aziz.*

(below) *King Faisal bin Abd el-Aziz kisses the Black Stone of Mecca, now sheathed in silver to protect it from the ravages of time. The Black Stone was placed at the corner of the Ka'aba by Mohammed himself.*

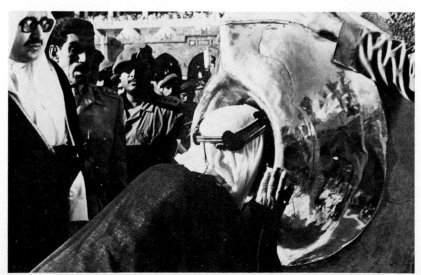

(above) *Jiddah was the main trading centre of Arabia when the city was ruled by the Sharif of Mecca and King Abd el-Aziz was determined not to risk the lives of foreigners there when he surrounded it in 1924. He chose to wait for its surrender rather than take the city by storm. This photograph shows the old Mecca Gate, now replaced by a modern highway.*

(below) *The Ka'aba at Mecca—centre of the Muslim world. The city was captured by Mohammed himself in 630 and since then has been the first holy city of Islam. At Mecca, everyone, from the King to his humblest subject, wears the same simple clothing, signifying that in the eyes of the Prophet all men are equal.*

(above) *Desert tribesmen of Asir province take coffee in the desert. Asir was formerly under the domain of the Sharif of Mecca, but became part of the Sa'udi Kingdom on the fall of the Hejaz in 1924.*

(below) *Relaxing in Taif, the mountain resort of the Hejaz. It is peaceful now but was the scene of the fierce beginning of the conquest of the province.*

The first oil concessions were signed in 1933, a year after the name Saudi Arabia was given to the kingdom. Here, King Abd el Aziz inspects a drilling rig at Dhahran, soon to become the oil centre of the world.

and south, into the Turkish provinces of Mesopotamia and into the tribes of the Arab peninsula. There were in addition a certain number of Wahhabi exiles living in Kuwait (as many as two hundred young or youngish men at one time) who were always willing to follow this amazing young prince in his adventures.

For Abd el-Aziz was obviously, from the earliest days, an astonishing phenomenon. He had an incisive mind and enough learning to support it—besides which he was an inveterate learner: he never stopped learning things to the day of his death. He had, as well, a most remarkable physique, wiry and powerful and resistant to untold fatigue: he could (like many Bedouin) live on practically nothing in case of need; and he was very tall, handsome, and possessed of a charm which became legendary throughout the desert and afterwards the world. He had strongly marked Semitic features, with a hooked nose and full lips, wonderfully expressive eyes and a voice which could range from a roar to a whisper like any great actor's. Actually he was only six feet three inches tall—De Gaulle might have made him look short—but this, which is well above the average in any country, is a towering height in Arabia. The entire House of Sa'ud, by the way, seems to have participated in this dominant tallness; at least, among the princes I have met, only two or three have been of average height. The others loom high and large over their contemporaries.

This prince, then, conceived the notion of reconquering his ancestral capital, with as much of its domain as he could manage, with his own slender resources, without backing or approval from any true centre of authority, and without having arranged anything in advance either with the local Nejdi tribes or with any other focus of power. It was one of the most madcap ventures ever undertaken and, as happens so rarely in life, it not only succeeded but led on to other triumphs—indeed to a series of triumphs without parallel in modern Arabian history.

Abd el-Aziz set out from Kuwait with about forty followers, all friends and Wahhabi, in the spring of 1902. He had had a little experience with serious fighting in 1900, when he commanded a small Bedouin force in support of the Sheikh of Kuwait against the Rashidi prince. Mohammed ibn Rashid had died in 1897; his nephew and successor was a Bedu leader in the field, but otherwise unqualified to govern or administer the considerable domain which his uncle had built up. Moreover, against the threat of Turkish encroachment, the British had at last made a treaty with Kuwait in 1899 which established a protectorate on the same terms as for the other states along the Gulf (Bahrein, for instance, or the states of the Perpetual Truce). The situation had therefore changed fairly radically in a few years, although nobody was to know that these changes would be, as they proved to be, so greatly in favour of the young Sa'udi prince.

He made his camel march at first rather slowly towards the south, picking up tribesmen adherents along the way and losing them almost as fast as he gained them. Without loot or the promise of loot there were few Bedouin who would stick long in one enterprise. Abd el-Aziz reached Riyadh, encircled it and them made his plan of surprise. Leaving most of his tribesmen recruits and others (under command of his brother Mohammed) in a palm grove south of the town, he took his forty chosen followers and worked his way around to the north, where there was a breach in the wall from the fighting of twelve years before. Here, after dark, it was no trick at all for the Sa'udi partisans to creep into the town and find their way to the citadel, where, they were informed, the Rashidi governor had the habit of sleeping for safety's sake, returning to his own house after the earliest prayer.

Here, in the house at the citadel gate, they gained entry by a ruse, locked all the women and servants up in one room, and then waited out the night on the roof, watching for the governor. When the Rashidi official appeared, early in the morning, the Sa'udi partisans rushed him and his escort; there was a brief, sharp clash, the Rashidi chief was killed, and within the hour Abd el-Aziz was being welcomed home to Riyadh by delegations of the citizens.

It was a signal triumph, made more remarkable and more lasting by the slowness of the Rashidi camp to wake up to its significance. The Rashidi prince of the day (whose name, as it happens, was also Abd el-Aziz) had little historical imagination and appears to have treated the episode lightly. He did not realize, among other things, the depths to which Wahhabi religious feeling could go, or the extent to which the House of Sa'ud was entwined with the tradition and the sincerest hopes of the Wahhabi faithful.

Abd el-Aziz, in later years known throughout the western world as 'Ibn Sa'ud', was a very different personage. He knew the Bedouin and the Wahhabi, being in the deepest sense both; and he had his own exceptional qualities of iron patience and steely courage, without which, indeed, his cause had been lost before it started.

His first task was to rebuild the walls of Riyadh solidly and fortify them with everything he could get; his next was to recruit and discipline a force from the south, amongst the tribes which had never really accepted the rule of the Rashidi or paid the tribal taxes to them. When Ibn Rashid was ready for an attack on Riyadh (which was not until the winter of 1902–1903) Abd el-Aziz was ready.

Indeed one of the Rashidi failings then and afterwards with Abd el-Aziz was a refusal or inability to concentrate. Ibn Rashid could not get out of his head the notion that Kuwait was his real enemy, and he wasted much time dawdling with his forces on the edges of Kuwait territory with a view to invasion, regardless of the fact that the principality was now under British protection. Then, when at intervals he remembered his enemy to the south, the astonishing Abd el-Aziz ibn Sa'ud, it was always after the Sa'udi had had a chance to fortify, train and grow stronger. Thus after three successive defeats on his invasions of Nejd, a year or so apart, Abd el-Aziz ibn Rashid had to retreat to his own territory in the Jebel Shammar.

Abd el-Aziz ibn Sa'ud seems to have been confident enough. One of his first acts as ruler of Riyadh in the summer of 1902 was to ask his father, the Imam Abd el-Rahman, to come to the capital from Kuwait. Abd el-Rahman was still (and would until death remain) the Imam of the Wahhabi, but he had abdicated the secular sovereignty a year before and now would have none of it: he came to Riyadh gladly, and was welcomed home, but he wanted the entire command and secular responsibility to fall upon Abd el-Aziz, which it did by both nature and arrangement. Abd el-Aziz was known as *Shuyukh*, plural of Sheikh, leader of the people, in those early years, but later adopted the style of 'Amir of Nejd', by which he was known for decades. For twenty-five years of this time the Imam Abd el-Rahman remained as his closest friend and adviser, taking precedence as head of the House of Sa'ud on all official occasions, but leaving government (*absolute* government, of course) in the hands of Abd el-Aziz. After a few months the new Amir brought his entire family from Kuwait—not his brothers only; they had been with him on the redeeming expedition—but all the wives and children of the entire family and all the faithful servants who had shared their wanderings.

Ibn Rashid's hesitations, as between Kuwait in the north and Nejd in the centre (that is, to his south) proved fatal to any idea of reconquest. Abd el-Aziz ibn Sa'ud was growing stronger every day. The Bedouin, who in those days smelled success as they could smell loot (and indeed the two were synonymous) flocked to him and he gave them, or many of them, some training, a good many weapons and some employment. The core of his forces remained Wahhabi townsmen or villagers, not nomads; this stable element, with its religious devotion to his cause, was the only one of its kind in the desert, and under such skilled leadership it was bound to be effective. The Bedouin came and went: at the month of Ramadhan, for example, the month-long daytime fast, they were likely to go home to their own tents and women, whatever the strategic situation might be, so as to 'fast in comfort', as Philby says. Until the formation of the *Ikhwan* (1912), the Brotherhood, no Bedouin tribesman had submitted to military discipline or the rule of a power beyond the tribe. This fluid element may have been large in numbers, but an astute commander would never count upon their being in the right place at the right time, or indeed any other time. In some of his many battles for twenty years Abd el-Aziz had loyal Bedouin support, and in large numbers; the ferocity of the Bedouin in battle was notorious, and contributed to the fear with which ordinary citizens regarded them; but there were other battles in which the tribesmen 'allies' (as they were correctly called) had faded away in large numbers or altogether, owing to dozens of reasons having, very often, nothing to do with war or politics.

The Amir Abd el-Aziz when he captured Riyadh was twenty-two years old by the accepted (conventional) date of his birth, November 24th, 1880. The precise date is uncertain. During the decade which followed his twenty-second birthday he made constant additions to his territory, not all of them by military force: indeed a great many tribal regions were glad to accept his rule. Before three years were up he had reconquered all the territory ruled by his grandfather Faisal before the debacle. From then on it was a steady progress towards the assimilation of all the provinces held by Sa'ud the Great at his greatest, including (1924) Mecca itself and the Hedjaz.

Until then there was a long, hard road to pursue, with the Rashidi family of Shammar as the constant enemy, with the Turks and the British and the Sharif of Mecca constantly interfering or opposing obstacles, and with the tribesmen who shifted as easily and suddenly as their sands. Abd el-Aziz, was indeed a Bedu by nature, and knew their herds and watering places, roads and habitual roaming grounds, as well as they did; he never spoke classical Arabic, but always the dialect of the central desert; and much of his lifelong triumph came from knowing the Bedouin as well as anybody could know them. But they were not trained to loyalty, except the blood-loyalty of the tribe, and at the sniff of unsuccess they faded away. It took consummate skill (and still does) to keep these nomads contented and on good terms with their central government.

Abd el-Aziz had one grand idea which dominated a large part of his life: that was, to make sedentary workers and citizens out of the nomads. It was a work of vast scale and could not be done in any one man's lifetime, but a beginning could be made. It was made with the foundation of the *Ikhwan* (Brotherhood) in 1912, which was an order of 'soldier-saints', as Philby calls them. They were young men from the tribes (different tribes) who for reasons of Wahhabi religious fervour were willing to settle in colonies, undergo military training and live according to the strictest rules of their very strict doctrine. The first of these colonies was at Artawiya, a group of wells in the desert, which rapidly grew into a town of 10,000 inhabitants, and Ghatghat, a similar centre, which had the enthusiastic support, so far as his resources extended, of the Amir. Abd el-Aziz made himself responsible for the wells and the mosque as well as for the military training, ammunition and equipment which were to make the *Ikhwan* into a striking force unique in modern Arabia. This—the military force—was in all likelihood only one of the Amir's aims in creating the *Ikhwan*, and not the principal one at that; he was sincerely interested in doing something to mitigate the insecurity of the Bedouin's lot, and to settle them on the land seemed the best way of doing so. Furthermore, his zeal as a Wahhabi never faltered, and he wanted these young men to be bulwarks of the faith. But, as it happened, they turned into a fanatical fighting force, one of the most determined (and ferocious) known to desert history, until only a few years later their very name struck terror into those who tilled the soil in a regular manner or dwelt in cities and villages. In the end their creator was forced to be also their destroyer; they had greatly aided his conquest of Arabia for a decade, but in the end they, too, had to go as an obstacle to unity.

In the meantime they were extremely useful. Some of Abd el-Aziz's campaigns in the first twenty-five years of his activity are astonishing in their swift success, their shrewdness in judging the enemy's weaknesses, their exploitation of favourable circumstance whenever it occurred. We have skimmed over a whole decade of tribal warfare (1902–1912) as being too complicated and too remote for one story; but the general tendency—victory to Abd el-Aziz—we have made clear. There were times when the young Amir had to recognize, for a certain time and place, some suzerainty of the Turks (as in the province of Qasim) but it never went beyond a formal or even ritualistic observance. The evidence is that Abd el-Aziz conceived himself to be quite independent of the Ottoman Empire and looked towards the earliest chance of proving it. It came in the spring of 1913 when, by a series of sharp flanking movements preceded by an attack on Hofuf, the capital, he cleared the whole Turkish occupying force out of the province of al-Hasa within the single month of March. Hasa, the fertile land, fertile in dates, corn and vegetables as well as livestock (and those beautiful little Hasawi donkeys!) now returned to the fold in the Wahhabi empire, from which the Turks had so easily detached it twenty-odd years before, on pretence of helping the Imam Abdullah against his brother Sa'ud.

Abd el-Aziz had now substantially renewed the family dominion over central Arabia with the exception of the Jebel Shammar, where the Rashidi clan exercised its independent rule with no thought of acknowledging an overlordship. There were gaps also in the west, and there is no doubt at all that the Amir's mind drifted towards Mecca and Medina, as was natural for any devout Arab, and he would not have been human if he had not reflected that these fair and holy cities had belonged to his forebears a century ago.

At this point in his career the great Arab had not only become an obsession for his Arab neighbours, up to and including Kuwait, but had aroused the interest—to say the least—of the external powers most concerned, that is, the British and Ottoman empires. The British had made the Persian Gulf 'a British lake', but on the firm and repeated declaration that they were only interested in the salt water and its immediate shores, open trade and the suppression of piracy. Nothing that happened in the interior of Arabia was of interest to London, according to this policy. Furthermore, everything concerning the Persian Gulf and its shores—the whole policy, in fact—came under the jurisdiction of the Government of Bombay operating under the Government of India at Delhi. This interposed two layers of authority between anything that might happen in the Amir's part of the world and the centre of the British Empire, with concomitant delays.

Nevertheless, he tried from an early stage of his career to get into some fruitful kind of exchange with the British. He realized that the *Turk* was the real enemy of his independence and it was his desire to prepare for his final struggle, if it was to come, by the aid of the British.

His first attempt, Philby tells us, came in 1904 when the Government of India for the first time installed a British Agent officially in Kuwait to watch over the freedom of that enclave from Turkish ambition. Abd el-Aziz had only been in precarious power for two years at the time, and he wanted the security of a British alliance, making his approach through his father, the Imam Abd el-Rahman. The reply was the stereotyped one—that the British were not interested in the interior of Arabia, but only in the Persian Gulf for trade purposes, and that H.M. Government had friendly relations with the Turks and did not wish to offend them.

Matters remained in this state for seven years, so far as we know, with Abd el-Aziz steadily enlarging and fortifying his realm and the British ignoring him. Then, in the spring of 1911, he dined with Captain William Shakespear, the new British Political Agent, in Kuwait. Captain Shakespear was the first Englishman or other European Abd el-Aziz had ever actually met in his life. The conversation was a repetition of what had gone before: Shakespear gave the Amir the same reply, Britain was not interested in anything but the Gulf, Britain had friendly relations with the Turks, etc., etc. But there was something else, something intangible, in this conversation, since it had consequences; perhaps Shakespear conveyed, without saying so, that he would present the Amir's suggestions and see what might happen. Perhaps—since he was a great one for instinct—Abd el-Aziz had instinctively liked and trusted the young British soldier. They were of the same age, just over thirty, and Shakespear had just returned from a month's foray into the desert, where he had lived with and liked the Bedouin: we may be sure that this aroused the interest and sympathy, or at least the curiosity, of the Amir. Later Shakespear, on a long journey in the desert, fortuitously met with Abd el-Aziz and a martial column and made his camp with them. On this occasion Captain Shakespear's diary has the entry: 'March 6, 1911. Camped with Ibn Sa'ud. Raining.'

There was considerable talk about Abd el-Aziz's plans, just the same. The Amir wanted—indeed, proposed—to drive the Turks out of Hasa province, their last foothold in Arabia, but he wished to be assured of British help in the event of an attack by sea, which he could not otherwise resist for lack of ships and fortifications. Shakespear undoubtedly made the usual reply and, whatever else was discussed, the fact is that Abd el-Aziz went ahead and drove the Turks out of Hasa two years later and the Ottoman Empire made no effort to attack by sea. British help had proved unnecessary.

In the meantime Shakespear made a dispatch from Kuwait to his immediate superior, Sir Percy Cox, the British Agent in Baghdad, who sent it on by the usual channels to Bombay, Delhi and eventually London. It was only in London that these communications from the

Persian Gulf got themselves transferred from the India Office to the Foreign Office; that side of Arabia was always the business of the Government of India, whereas the other side (the Red Sea) was the business of the Foreign Office. The division had arisen because the main authority on the Red Sea (Hejaz and Yemen) was at least nominally the Ottoman Empire (foreign) whereas the local sheikhs and princelings on the Persian Gulf were only Arabs (somehow not so foreign, I suppose, and near enough to India to be interesting).

The reply, although signed by many men in many offices (as comment or 'minutes' on the original dispatch), was in effect the same—a refusal to take part in Arabian affairs, although more than one official saw that the Amir might some day be useful if the Turks became too difficult.

In February, 1914, Shakespear set out on his longest Arabian journey, from Kuwait to Akaba by way of Riyadh (a very long detour indeed—it must have been for the express purpose of meeting the Amir again). He camped outside the Sa'udi capital—then a city of mud huts, even the fortress, palace and mosque being of the prevailing material—and went in frequently to see Abd el-Aziz, with whom his talk was along the same lines as before. After his journey he went to England on leave.

Then the 1914 war broke out without, so far as the Persian Gulf was concerned, any serious warning, and the British found themselves without Arabic-speaking officers to deal with the situation. Above all they needed Shakespear, the only one who was friendly with Abd el-Aziz, and he was recalled to the Gulf from England as fast as possible. He did not reach Arabia again until the last days of 1914.

Abd el-Aziz's whole position had, of course, changed, and both sides —Turks and British—were now seeking his favour. This pair of enemies had signed a treaty of friendship shortly before the outbreak of war (March 9th, 1914), ratified by the British on June 3rd, 1914, but never by the Turks, in which the whole of southern Arabia from the Yemen to the Qatar peninsula was given to the British to 'protect', including territory in the hinterland (the Bureimi oasis among others) which had always belonged to the Sa'udi dynasty and continued to do so. It was a brazen and puzzling affair, since Abd el-Aziz was never consulted, and neither Turk nor British had any claim to the territory. This 'friendship treaty' was to have gone into effect on October 31st, 1914, the day on which Turkey actually declared war against Great Britain.

Meanwhile Shakespear arrived in Arabia, met the Amir at Kapsi, his war camp below Artawiya in the desert, and between them they drew up a treaty along the lines Abd el-Aziz had always stipulated. The British recognized the independence of the Sa'udi dominions— no longer with any reservations about Turkish suzerainty—and Abd el-Aziz was pledged to engage in an armed struggle with Ibn Rashid (which he was already doing) and to refrain from attacking the Sharif of Mecca, whom the British wished to take under their wing and eventually did. The Sa'udi monarch would receive a subsidy of 5,000 sovereigns a month in gold (about $300,000 a year) for his added expenses, plus a certain quantity of arms and ammunition. This was not much in comparison to the money which was soon to be lavished on the Sharif of Mecca and other Arab chieftains in the west, but it was an essential contribution to the impoverished war chest of the Sa'udi.

Shakespear sent the treaty on to Sir Percy Cox in Baghdad and waited with the Amir for the reply. During this time the Sa'udi and Rashidi forces clashed at a field called Jirrab, halfway between Artawiya and Zilfi, where Shakespear, directing the fire of the Sa'ud's two old Turkish cannon, was killed. He wore full British uniform in this engagement, taking part against the urgent wishes of Abd el-Aziz, who deeply regretted his loss. The battle was not a victory for either side, but the Rashidi lost their camp and equipment to a marauding Wahhabi detachment, while the Sa'udi were unable to keep the field through the speedy retirement of their Bedouin levies. In the result, indecisive as it was between Arabs, the British gained a point, because Ibn Rashid was unable to operate for some time against the Indian Army's invasion (through Kuwait) of Mesopotamia.

In a sense the Sa'udi sat out the war, engaging in no serious hostilities even against the Rashidi, their hereditary prey, although they did harass them fairly constantly in a minor way. And of course, in deference to British wishes, they did not attack the Sharif of Mecca, who from 1916 onwards was in full revolt against the Ottoman Empire with the support of the Arab Bureau in Cairo and its emissary, T. E. Lawrence—a whole separate wing of British policy, distinct from that which dealt with the Persian Gulf. Indeed there were times when the Persian Gulf authority (Sir Percy Cox as Agent, later High Commissioner to Baghdad), and the Arab Bureau in Cairo, Lawrence's superiors, acted as if they were different or even rival powers, so great was the gap between them.

Anybody who reads the correspondence between Sir Henry McMahon in Cairo and the Sharif Hussein in Mecca must see that, in spite of cautious language, the British were giving Hussein every reason to suppose that he might, by victorious assistance in the war, become King of all the Arabs. Such promises are not specifically made, but there is a promise (clearly outlined with frontiers) of independence for the Arabs of Syria, Palestine and Iraq, and Hussein was free to take the implication that he, as the Arab leader, could rule all this after the war in independent sovereignty. The existence of contradictory promises to the Zionists and to the French was not known to Mecca and the Sharif had some justification for his dreams of grandeur. The rumours that filled the desert were not welcome at Nejd, where the House of Sa'ud ruled a much larger and more warlike territory than Hussein and treasured its own independence.

Even so, Lawrence's meteoric campaign up the railroad from the Hejaz to Damascus distracted the attention of the British (and of everybody else) from Abd el-Aziz during the second half of the war, and it was easy enough for the Wahhabi to build up their resources and wait. They were uneasy, to be sure; and Abd el-Aziz made Cox well aware of it. In 1917 a new mission to Riyadh from Baghdad (which had in the meantime been captured from the Turks) was carefully, even studiously prepared, with enough members to give it weight, and Cox put at its head Harry St. John Philby, who had been his own confidential secretary in charge of the preparation.

Philby arrived in Riyadh and met Abd el-Aziz on November 30, 1917. It was the beginning of a lifelong friendship in the course of which the Englishman was to renounce his own government's service in order to be of use to Abd el-Aziz, whom he quite simply worshipped, and eventually became a Muslim for (so far as one can discern) much the same reason.

Philby spent many hours with Abd el-Aziz every day—34 out of the first 132 hours after his arrival, he says—and conceived for him that high opinion which was afterwards to be fortified in decades of experience. His 'mission' faded away, one man in this direction and the other in that, until there was nobody in it but himself to the end of the war.

The proposal first agreed upon between Philby and Abd el-Aziz involved an immediate attack on the Rashidi in Jebel Shammar (specifically on Hail, their capital), for which the Sa'udi would receive augmented funds and weapons—50,000 gold sovereigns for each of the three months allotted to the campaign; 10,000 modern rifles with ample ammunition; recruits from the Arab prisoners of war captured by the British from the Turks; and some other advantages. Then

Philby, in rather a mysterious way, persuaded the Amir to give him an armed escort across the desert to the Hejaz so as to talk to the Sharif of Mecca—by now King of the Hejaz—about co-operation in the war. David Howarth, in *The Desert King,* says that Philby's private aspirations were responsible for this futile attempt to cajole Hussein. Mr. Howarth says:

> The fact was that he already pictured himself as a famous explorer, and longed for the achievement of having crossed Arabia from coast to coast; and he twisted his wartime duty to suit this personal ambition.

This could be the literal truth—Philby was an extraordinary character and could convince himself of almost anything—but it had the result of holding up Sa'udi operations in the desert for the whole winter, during which the situation in the war changed fundamentally and the Amir's services were no longer needed. We who fly from Jiddah to Riyadh by jet plane in an hour may find it hard to realize that it took well over two weeks (nearer three) to travel the same distance at a fairly swift pace by camel.

And, furthermore, Hussein had no desire to talk to Philby. He sent Hogarth (the celebrated David Hogarth of the Arab Bureau in Cairo, who was now one of his advisers) down to Jiddah to see the visitor, but then detained him in the Hejaz indefinitely and finally consented to send him out (for reasons of his own 'safety') to Cairo only. Philby made his way to Cairo, to Bombay and thence again through the Persian Gulf to his starting point in Nejd.

Lawrence's campaign up the railroad to Damascus had been successful; Allenby had captured Jerusalem; the war with the Turks, at least, was almost over. Philby encouraged the Amir, even so, without British artillery or other material help (advancing him £20,000 on his own authority for camels and local equipment) into an unsuccessful attempt to conquer the Rashidi and Hail. That failure was enough for the Wahhabi; they would not move again until they had some assurance of success. The end of the war found them where they were before, with the added anxiety that the Sharif of Mecca, now King of the Hejaz, was openly claiming the sovereignty of the entire Arab world in the Middle East, including the entire peninsula with Palestine, Syria, Iraq as well.

It was at this point that Abd el-Aziz sent his second son, Prince Faisal (now King) to England on a journey of good will and good wishes on the victory. Faisal was only thirteen; Philby went with him; among other things, they paid a visit to old Charles Doughty in the country. For the boy Faisal it was the beginning of an interminable series of visits to the West and to other foreign countries, in which he has spent a significant part of his life.

The growing importance of the Amir's other sons was due in part to the death of his eldest, Prince Turki, in the epidemic of Spanish influenza at the end of the war. Turki had been closely associated with Abd el-Aziz and was treated as his heir apparent and—when necessary—substitute; he commanded the armed forces during any absence of his father, for example. This left only juniors who were, in fact, very junior: Sa'ud, the second son, to be proclaimed Crown Prince in a few years, and Faisal, the third son, so early broken in to his long experience of diplomacy.

By 1920, without the British artillery and other material aid he had been promised, the Amir was ready to annihilate his last remaining rival in the desert, the House of Rashid. By now it was crumbling indeed—the brothers and cousins had murdered each other with persistence since the death of their grandfather Mohammed—and a final family quarrel laid the whole area (the Jebel Shammar, its tribes and its capital, Hail) open to Abd el-Aziz. He won easily without British support; in the hour of victory he distinguished himself by great clemency, indeed chivalry, towards the princes of that family which, once loyal supporters of his own house, had been the enemy for almost half a century. Rashidi princes remained for decades as friends, pensioners and ornaments of the court at Riyadh.

It is difficult to understand what the British were thinking during all this time about Abd el-Aziz. They must have known, from their Persian Gulf reports, that his power was great and growing, that nobody in the desert could stand against him; and yet they were curiously hypnotized by T. E. Lawrence and his fixation on the Sharifian (Hashemite) family. In this illusion or delusion they continued for some time after the war, until the Sharif himself, by megalomaniac procedures (including eventually the proclamation of himself, unsupported, as Caliph of Islam), alienated those who wished him well. Churchill (with the advice of Lawrence) 'interpreted' the wartime promises into a series of separate states, two of them given as kingdoms to Hussein's sons, and the Sharif, or King of the Hejaz, was left fuming with indignation in Mecca.

The cessation of his subsidy from Great Britain (1924) threw the Amir into a predicament both financial and political. He had not liked the Iraq-Transjordan creations, which gave him undefined frontiers with the Sharif's sons; he had an undefined frontier with the Sharif himself, and his *Ikhwan*, his Bedouin-Wahhabi 'soldier saints', were spoiling for a fight. Without the five thousand sovereigns he drew every month from Britain, the monarch of the desert would be unable to sustain and restrain them or the nomad raiders in his territory. He had been subsidized as a war-time measure and for two specific objectives: to attack Ibn Rashid and *not* to attack the Sharif. He had done the first, without British material aid: he was sovereign of the entire desert except the Hejaz; and when the British wished to withdraw their war-time subsidy he quite naturally concluded that this was their consent to an attack on the Hejaz.

The attack followed promptly upon Hussein's proclamation (early 1924) of his own caliphate, which was very poorly received throughout Islam. Abd el-Aziz could have taken the Hejaz at any time for years past, but now that it was ripe he asked for an assembly of the wise men (Ulema) and elders to decide. The message they sent out to Islam was signed by Prince Faisal, who was then only eighteen.

The conquest of the Hejaz was quick and easy, marred by a bloodthirsty beginning at Taif, the mountain resort, where the Ikhwan went mad and killed some three or four hundred non-combatants. The looting and other outrages at Taif, although not repeated, gave the Brotherhood a terrible reputation all along the Red Sea coast and made subsequent advances easy, although the Amir was cruelly disappointed at their conduct and perhaps even then began to think that they were too fanatical for further usefulness. Jiddah (under Ali, another of Hussein's sons) held out for a long, inactive siege, but the Amir was determined on clemency and would not push matters. In the end, without more bloodshed or ill-feeling, he got the whole of the Hejaz and with it the province of Asir, to which the Hejaz had long asserted sovereign right without administering it.

Abd el-Aziz behaved with great circumspection at this crucial period. Obviously the Ikhwan had to be restrained; he had been at Riyadh (over two weeks away by fast camel) when they got out of hand at Taif, and he never ceased to regret it; he was conscious of the foreigners in Jiddah, consuls, merchants and all, and would not take the city by storm even though he could have done so easily; he merely surrounded it and starved it out. When Ali ibn Hussein finally surrendered (at the request of the inhabitants) the Wahhabi prince allowed him and his family to go in peace—ultimately to the life of British pensioners on Cyprus—and agreed that the dreaded Ikhwan would never be allowed to enter the port city.

At every step Abd el-Aziz seems to have been aware of the importance of the foreigners and of foreign opinion, which—for an Arab of
his region and lineage—was something quite new. When he had
captured the whole of the Hejaz, he faced the necessity of administering a territory and population very different from any he had governed
before. The patriarchal—and virtually theocratic—monarchy of the
desert had to make accommodations to reality in this Red Sea coastal
plain where centuries of traffic with foreigners had affected every part
of life. The Wahhabi who flocked to the Hejaz wanted to enforce the
whole of their puritanical system (abstention from tobacco, alcohol,
even coffee; prohibition of silks and fine linen; prayer compulsory
five times a day; and numerous other severe rules) upon city Arabs
who were not, and never could be, used to it. Between his desert
followers and his new subjects Abd el-Aziz had to use great skill,
diplomacy and persuasion. The Wahhabi prevailed, of necessity, for a
while, but after 1927 the King succeeded in sending most of them
back to their native deserts (beginning with the Ikhwan troops who
had been such a problem) and allowing the Hejaz population to slip
gradually into its normal way of living. The breadth of mind and
tolerant spirit shown by Abd el-Aziz at this period must have been
natural to him, an element in his genius, for we find little to account
for it in his environment. The fanatical Wahhabi (for example, the
chiefs of the *Ikhwan*) were often at variance with the actions and beliefs
of their King. They suffered his benevolence without approving it;
they thought him weak to the infidel (and by infidel they meant also
those Muslims who did not agree with them); they were puzzled by a
great many of his firm, continued and consistent policies towards his
new subjects and his neighbours. In a word, their disagreement was
fundamental, their incomprehension nearly total, their ultimate
rebellion a certainty. Having been made up out of religious preaching
and military discipline, they had room for little or nothing else, and
their headlong course (after the conquest of the Hejaz, which made
them prouder than ever) could have been foreseen.

Abd el-Aziz stayed in the Hejaz for two full years after its surrender,
and during that time the desert tribes which had joined the Ikhwan
grew more and more restive. They actually did not dare raid other
tribes of the realm, since the new ruler had so fiercely forbidden it;
they did worse: they raided across the border into Kuwait and Iraq,
which by now were fully protected by the British Air Force, creating
an international complication just when a climax had been reached in
progress towards orderly government, centralization and peace in the

greater part of Arabia. In the end Abd el-Aziz had to annihilate the Ikhwan, although as usual he behaved with the greatest chivalry towards its captured leaders and their families.

The firm (at times ruthless) creation of order in the Hejaz was one of the King's immediate achievements there, and he reaped a harvest from it by way of the pilgrims. The practice of robbing pilgrims had been for a very long time a source of livelihood to the Bedouin of the Hejaz borders, and every sort of extortion had been customary even in the market places of the towns. Abd el-Aziz came down upon all this traffic with the severity of an avenging deity. The man who could be so high-minded and chivalrous about a conquered opponent— who could weep when a vanquished enemy kissed his hand—was as remorseless as fate towards the robbers in Islam's Holy Land. As a result, within a few months perfect order had been restored in that agelong abode of thievery; the word of it travelled all over the Muslim world; the numbers of pilgrims sharply increased, and in the first year after the conquest there were a hundred thousand of them, a number not known before. The increase since then has been constant, so that an enormous part of the medical, police and transport services of the greatly enriched kingdom has gone to care for it. There is, of course, an entry fee, and the revenues of Abd el-Aziz went up quickly after he took the Hejaz; but aside from this fee (which is not heavy for the individual—it seems to me that I paid seven dollars) there are, and have been since the Sa'udi took over, no further exactions. The pilgrim pays for food and lodging, as he would anywhere, although even these are made very easy for him in the present opulent state of Arabia. Transport is lavish, the roads in this region are superb, the hostels even in the most crowded seasons are adequate: all has changed. Abd el-Aziz even when he became King did not have great resources—indeed he continued for years to be very short of money—but he could and did ensure the one essential thing, which was that the devout Muslim could make his pilgrimage to Mecca, as the Koran enjoined, without risking everything he possessed or could carry, and even too often, his life itself.

The return of Philby into the King's existence occurred at this period (that is, after the conquest of Mecca and during the siege of Jiddah—1925). This odd man had resigned from the British government service after a session in Transjordan (as Representative to the Amir Abdullah) and one in Iraq: he did not like imperialism at all, he said, and we believe him, but we believe chiefly that he longed for Arabia and Abd el-Aziz. His instinct informed him that here he could find a career of satisfaction to himself: he could explore and explain and expatiate to his heart's content, with (on the whole) the consent and approval of the sovereign ruler, and there were no rivals: he was practically the only westerner who knew anything about modern Arabia or the House of Sa'ud, and certainly the only one who could write copiously about it. This he did for another thirty years or more, a stunning example of concentration, and although he was by no means a great writer or thinker, the simple facts that he accumulated and passed on were worth the effort. His books are for the most part little known in Arabia and most of them have been banned there anyhow; England and the English-speaking world have almost ignored him; but, even so, Philby, all by himself, has carved out his place. It would be impossible to consider these subjects at all without giving full consideration to Philby as writer, as influence, as inveterate meddler (perhaps) and ultimately as historical force. The very fact that the Americans are in Arabia for the extraction of petroleum and its by-products is partly traceable to Philby's influence: that in itself is enough.

It is quite clear that the King liked him—liked him enough to put up with some kinds of impertinence which would not have been permitted in others. Abd el-Aziz was obviously a very instinctive being, and perhaps he felt that in this peculiar Englishman there was something he could trust to the limit. Kings have few they can trust. Philby quite often disagreed with His Majesty and said so bluntly; there were times when the relations between them were clouded by such disagreements; and yet Abd el-Aziz always came back to this hero-worshipper who was not afraid of his hero. I have had various ideas about Philby's extraordinary career in Arabia, and one is, quite simply, that he had a talent for the Arabic language. Those of my friends who knew him (and there are quite a few) say that he was by no means a master of the language, and yet he was fluent and easy in it, and never had the slightest difficulty expressing himself. King Abd el-Aziz never spoke good (or literary) Arabic in his life—always the language of Nejd—and it must have seemed quite astonishing to him, at first, to find a foreigner who could talk his own language better than he could. In addition to this, I detect in Philby's writing a distinct, if crotchety personality, a tang of originality and obstinacy (along with quarrelsome, litigious dispositions) which must have made him altogether different from the sauve myrmidons of a court. The King saw it and felt it, and as the years wore on he came to depend upon Philby's presence. I do not say that he was particularly influenced by Philby on great matters—there were others, such as Abdullah Sulaiman and the Sheikh Hafiz Wabha, perhaps Yussuf Yassin, who carried more weight—but he liked to have Philby there, perhaps to consult, perhaps merely to talk to from time to time. The fact that Philby would not accept any form of employment, appointment, honours or emoluments may have had something to do with the King's regard. For specific purposes—an exploration: a specific journey such as the one recorded in his *Land of Midian*—he would willingly accept the King's bounty in the way of a purse for, say, two or three thousand golden sovereigns as expenses—but he never became an employee, a functionary of the State, or a pensioner.

He really was a most eccentric man, and readers of his work will have noted long ago that he had veins of superstition, credulousness and sheer insanity along with his robust common sense and knowledge of the world. He could spin webs of fantasy about numbers, for instance—that such a name combined with another made such a number, which coincided with another number, which in turn coincided with another, so as to form a sort of rhyming or conjunction across the wilderness of human history. I find this sort of thing hard to follow, since the pattern of destiny has never seemed simple or in the least arithmetical to me, but Philby believed.

Most of all, however, he believed in Abd el-Aziz and the emerging greatness of Arabia, a faith which sustained him for decades and in fact in itself goes far to tell us why Abd el-Aziz kept him on the string, so to speak, until the very end. It is a solace, perhaps even a form of happiness, for those who carry great responsibilities in this world to find belief—that is, personal belief, a belief in one's own person. This is what Philby had for Abd el-Aziz, possibly for thirty-six years, anyhow for about thirty years of that time.

On his return to Arabia he was not dignified by any British government title or position. In fact, having resigned from all that, he was the accredited selling agent for the Ford Motor Company and the Singer Sewing Machine Company, as well as some others, to which he added a few more as time went on. He was evidently not at all bad at this form of activity and continued in it for years. Arabia was already (in the 1920's) starved for consumer goods, and these gadgets and contrivances were readily accepted. As time passed Philby's friendship with Abd el-Aziz grew more solid and there were years when he spent almost his entire time at the court in Riyadh, going through a routine which he confessed to be unutterably boring (the same every day, the endless receptions to the tribesmen and the vast

meals with countless guests), but with intervals spent in exploring
the desert and writing books about it. His books, mostly unread, piled
up in the libraries but are a treasure-trove today for anybody interested
in the subject. They repeat themselves (God, how they repeat themselves!) and they almost always start out with a recognizable design
which is somehow lost *en route*; they meander and divagate; and whenever the author has a chance to quarrel with another author on any
small point he takes it with glee. Philby's wonderful opportunities
were not equalled by his talent, which was almost negligible; seldom
have such beautiful materials been wasted on such an inferior artist.
T. E. Lawrence (the bane of Philby's existence, so much so that he
puts the word Colonel in quotation marks, 'Colonel', when referring
to him) made immortality out of an episode; Philby, out of a whole
lifetime of devotion, has produced books which induce boredom and
irritation first of all, and only evoke interest afterwards because of
the facts which they indubitably contain, even though these must
always be counter-checked with other sources when possible.

We do not find Philby's influence affecting anything whatsoever
in the internal government of Arabia: Abd el-Aziz needed no counsel
in such matters. He knew the country, the land, the people; nobody
ever had a new fact to tell him. The tribes were his lifeblood and he
felt them rather than knew them. He was a blood relative to most of
them. With foreign matters he was less acquainted although, by some
miracle, far more acquainted than anybody else in his kingdom.

The importance of Philby arose from his ability to make the King
realize that foreigners could be honest and friendly, that they could
be beneficent, that they did not on the whole wish any ill to the Arabs,
that they would tell the truth when obliged to do so and that their
general scheme of things was decent enough, as human arrangements
go. The King's readiness to accept all this, in spite of his narrow
Wahhabi training, is a proof of his own historical genius. In one
great critical moment of his reign, socially and economically, he
accepted Philby's advice—that is, for the exploitation of the petroleum
resources of the Eastern Province, embodied in an agreement which,
with substantial amendments, remains today.

One word more about the King and Philby: we must always
remember that the King did not know very many foreigners. He had
met Shakespear, Cox and Philby; he had heard of a number of others;
he obviously was not attracted to the flamboyant legend of Lawrence,
the upholder of his enemies. He met the Americans in the 1930's,
during the exploration for oil—'By God, I like the man!' he said of

Tom Barger—and it seems that they got on quite well. Their ignorance was mutual, their liking instinctive. Amongst the American oil men I have met great esteem and even reverence for King Abd el-Aziz.

He aged, as we have seen earlier, with enormous dignity and universal respect. During the years some changes had occurred in his own character and physique; he was occasionally subjected to illness or fatigue, to which he had been a stranger for most of his existence; and Philby says he was disturbed, uneasy, over the fact that his wives no longer became pregnant as frequently as before. The King had, as is widely known, a large number of wives in succession, although never more than the Koranic four at any one time; indeed it is said that he had in all 'three hundred wives'. This seems a mere echo of the Old Testament tradition that King Solomon had that number of wives; it seems a little too apposite to be historical. There is no doubt, just the same, that the harem played a vast part in the King's life and although his attachments were fleeting they were at times strong. One of his wives remained a lifelong friend and an inhabitant of the palace decades after their divorce; and so far as companionship goes, we have already observed that his beloved sister's was the most enduring of all; he was at all times deeply susceptible to the charms and solaces of the women's quarters. His sexual prowess was phenomenal through the greater part of his life, and although he obeyed the Koranic restrictions he also availed himself of other privileges, such as concubines (official) and slaves. If David Howarth is correct in his book, *The Desert King*, Abd el-Aziz had four wives, four concubines and four slaves at any one time as his normal quota of bed companions. No matter how often they changed, this was the rule. (I have never asked questions about such things myself—I think Arabs are profoundly embarrassed by them, and it is better to restrict the questioning to what is necessary on the scale of external life.)

The King grew older, and the last period of his life was characterized by two symbolic events: the crushing of the *Ikhwan* in the late 1920's; the signing of the oil concessions in the 1930's. Both we have already surveyed; both were great things. In the second world war he found himself in the midst of a court which was as a general thing pro-German in feeling, and surrounded by agents of all the powers; but so far as I can tell he kept a generally pro-Allied course throughout, although not to the extent of risking his kingdom's existence in any premature pro-Allied demonstration. That he did, in the end, declare war against Germany and its allies was a mere pretext, in reality, to get his country into the initial stages of the United Nations, at that time (1945) restricted to the 'democratic' or 'anti-Fascist' powers.

His visits to Roosevelt and Churchill (after Yalta, 1945) were part of this process, and constituted the only time in his life that he had any first-hand experience of western diplomacy on its own ground.

The last decade of the great King's life was perhaps shadowed by new problems of wealth and responsibility, although I am not convinced by the theory that he was unhappy over them. Of course it was new and strange to have the vast revenues of oil exploitation pouring out from the Eastern Province when the world war was over. The King had a full decade of this unimaginable wealth. He did not himself spend a great deal of it, although he did indulge in a little building in Riyadh and elsewhere; but his sons and grandsons spent money in the most prodigal manner not only in Arabia (where his son Sa'ud never stopped building palaces) but all over Europe and America. There was as yet no concept of a budget, no feeling that this wealth belonged to the people, and even no proper system of accounting for sums disbursed. As a result the last days of the King's life may have been clouded by the fear that too much good fortune had endangered his whole family; Mr. Howarth certainly says so. I have not received any clear confirmation of this from persons who knew him well. He may have had religious compunctions over the luxury which, as he well knew, was spreading throughout his enormous family; he may have deplored the character most evident in the new-rich; he might even have felt some nostalgia for the old days and ways. Certainly he told Philby (and others) that he had never been so happy in his entire life as in the desert during the first period of combat for the throne. It may have been only nostalgia for his youth. We do not know. We know that he insisted on what he wanted and got it during those final years of wealth—he wanted a railroad, for example, having seen one on his visit to Egypt, and he got it (Dhahran to Riyadh), which in contemporary conditions in the desert is growing less useful, although it had an active decade or so. Motor cars and other properties were his for the asking; there was really nothing much, except youth and strength, that he could not have. I do not think we are justified in conjecturing that wealth itself made him unhappy, or that the behaviour of his new-rich descendants gave him any sense of 'dishonour', as Mr. Howarth calls it. After all, to King Abd el-Aziz this great annual flood of wealth was his own, a personal revenue from a

74

personal property, and he had no reason to deplore it or to indulge in the complications of a modern western conscience.

He died in Taif on November 9th, 1953, and was buried without ceremony at Riyadh, according to Wahhabi custom, in an unmarked grave. Certainly none of his countrymen since the Prophet Mohammed has made such a difference in Arabia.

5   Prince Faisal

THE present King is a contemporary examplar of the qualities which made King Abd el-Aziz what he was. By this I do not mean that he is exactly like his father—who could be?—but that an inheritance is obvious from the elements, not from their combination: that is, if the old King were Faisal's age he would be much more like Faisal than like himself. He was the forerunner, the great forerunner, but it is Faisal himself who is the King of Arabia. To the best of my knowledge and belief the old King never really felt at home out of the desert, and although this is most of Arabia, it is not all; Faisal is at home also in the cities, in the modern army, in the oil encampments, at a modern press conference, in the airplanes he studies and likes, among the students whom he welcomes and greatly favours, in the world of Islam and in the world of those whom his father would certainly have called the infidels (as Faisal does too, with a difference).

Whatever I have to say about the King must go under my own responsibility—as I said in the foreword to this book. I have talked to the King at length, of course, and he has at times been rather willing to talk, but at other times his mind was on other matters: he knew I was to write a book but he really did not see why I had to bother him about it. He has had grave preoccupations during this decade when I have been privileged to talk with him. On many occasions I have felt in Faisal's presence that he regarded the process of question and answer as futile, since everything of importance is too big and complex to be questioned or answered. At times I felt, also, that he instinctively resented a foreign inquisition into matters which were, after all, his own and exclusively his own. I kept on bothering him about things which were perpetually swirling in his own mind but about which he did not wish to speak for any public at all, Arab or foreign.

Nevertheless he did talk to me enough to give me a picture in some depth—a *quadro*, in Renaissance Italian, that is, something which is a composition and can be seen in a frame, a square—most often when he did not intend to do so. His mind, very great, pure and narrow, was never made to accept or even to discern the indiscriminate cosmopolitanism of my own. I found more comprehension, actually, in the Dalai Lama of Tibet, so young and frightened, who had never been outside his native mountains when he came to India, and yet was old and brave in his conversations with me when he was nineteen. And of course I remember Mr. Gandhi, in the last days of his life, speaking of an American lady photographer as 'the torturer'. What he meant was nothing unkind to her. What he meant was that she was always there and always taking pictures and (in spite of herself) too often interrupting his work. It is true that she took the best pictures ever taken of Mr. Gandhi, but he did not live to see them.

The King was always immensely King to me. This is the way he lives—it is the custom of the country. His father did the same, surrounded by guards, slaves and courtiers, an immense crowd of clients at the gate, a multitude of (in the Roman sense) 'suitors'. Faisal never at any moment talked to me as if he were not the absolute monarch: he never descended from that level. I explain this and even expatiate upon it, because it will serve to show how and why most of what I say about him comes, not from himself, but from others—from his sons, cousins, uncles and friends.

It is in this sense that I reiterate that the responsibility for all statements is mine, not his.

In the first place, my own impressions of this noble King are not the same as those of many who know him. He is said to regret his inability to drive a car himself (a friend told me); his inability to wander at will among the people in the *souk* (another friend); his inability to talk freely to foreigners (another friend); or his sealed-up and impregnable quality, as is usual with royalties, when he travels abroad.

These, as expressions of regret, are true and I have no doubt of it. But it is indeed a very long time since this King has been able to wander freely, unknown, amongst the populace of his own or any

77

other country. By now he must have grown with the decades. The desire of royal personages to mingle with the population has produced countless stories through the ages, and hardly any of them can be, according to common sense, what really happened. The only one that convinces us, mostly by language, is the one in *Henry V* when the King wanders through his sleeping troops on the eve of battle and talks to them. They do not know him, of course (an essential, condition of all these stories). Pistol says to him, at the start: 'Discuss unto me: art thou officer, or art thou base, common and popular?'

After several such exchanges with other soldiers the King is asked by an English soldier (there are English, Irish and Welsh) whether his commander has told his thoughts to the King.

The King replies: 'No; nor is it meet that he should. For though I speak it to you, I think the King is but a man as I am; the violet smells to him as it doth to me; the element shows to him as it does to me; all his senses have but human conditions; his ceremonies laid by, in his nakedness he appears but a man; and though his affections are higher mounted than ours, yet, when they stoop, they stoop with the like wing.'

The King goes on to speak of fear, which, if a King should show it, would 'dishearten his army', and the English soldier rambles on about how he would rather be anywhere but here, and if the King were up to his neck in the river Thames he would rather be there with the King than here on the hillside on the battle's eve.

Henry V says: 'By my troth, I will speak my conscience of the King: I think he would not wish himself anywhere but where he is.'

This, in substance, is what I have come to feel about King Faisal. He would not wish himself anywhere but where he is. This is his nature, which happens to coincide with historical destiny in its highest sense. He knows where he is and what he is, and what he has to do. He will do it. It is difficult to see what power on earth will keep him from doing it.

Now, of course, all these stories I hear about his desire to live otherwise and commune with the people in all countries must be true. I never did doubt them, even years ago when other Arabian princes were a public joke from the North Pole to the South. They had untold dollars and hardly knew the meaning of one. I had heard all those stories long before I went down to Arabia from Cairo in March, 1960. After ten minutes with Faisal (then Crown Prince and Prime Minister) in Riyadh in that month I knew that these were the transitory aspects of a strange and new phenomenon, and that Faisal represented the

78

truth, perhaps not only on his own sect or reign or ancestry, but of the Prophet Mohammed himself.

2

Faisal ibn el-Abd el-Aziz was born on May 17th, 1906, in the old royal palace at Riyadh, uniting the two lines of Sa'udi and Wahhabi ancestry which between them had moulded the history of the past century and a half for a great part of the Arabian peninsula. The empire or kingdom thus created by military and religious forces was still in formation and had, in fact, no formal name or style as yet beyond that the term of 'Nejd' as used for the original Wahhabi sheikhdom. ('Nejd and Its Dependencies' was a much later style, but there was no satisfactory term for the Sa'udi realm until the Kingdom of Sa'udi Arabia was proclaimed in 1932.)

The young prince was left without a mother very early, and at her death he passed for some years from his father's household to that of his maternal grandfather and grandmother, who brought him up during the childhood years which, ending at eleven or twelve, contain all the regular education considered necessary among the Arabs at the time. Faisal undoubtedly memorized the Koran as other boys did (they memorize aloud, under conditions which have seemed to me to tax them severely, but they do remember). In addition to this obligatory and basic task, which includes reading, writing and literature itself, Prince Faisal had an advantage not shared with his contemporaries: that is, the talk and teaching of his own grandfather, Sheikh Mohammed Abd el-Wahhab, descended from the great reformer of the same name, and almost equally renowned throughout Arabia for his learning, his skill in argument and his power in preaching. Sometimes observers have said that much of King Faisal's ability to argue with the *ulema,* the learned men of the Faith who are so influential in Arabia, comes from his youthful indoctrination or, perhaps even more, from the very memory of his grandfather: certainly he has been very successful in persuading the *ulema* to accept what in their minds constitutes innovation. (Innovation itself, in the orthodox and conservative Wahhabi mind, is regarded as dangerous.)

New things were inescapable in the early part of this century beginning with the fire-arms which made conquests possible, and the contact with the outside world established through the Red Sea and the Persian Gulf had its effects even in the central desert. When the first world war was over, Prince Faisal, at twelve, had completed the

Koranic education which was all his father had received, and which, beyond a doubt, constituted all the old King considered necessary. The thin-faced, thoughtful boy who had been brought up in a different atmosphere from that of the palace must have struck his father as being intellectually different from the others, just the same, because it was from this very early age that Abd el-Aziz began to consider Faisal as his emissary abroad, his representative to the foreigners. The Prince was, in fact, only thirteen when he made his first journey to Europe, accompanied by 'a suitable delegation' as Philby calls it (in *Arabian Jubilee*). The most suitable part of the delegation was probably Philby himself, who, although still in the British service at the time (1919) was becoming more and more devoted to Arabia and the Arabs. The young Prince was to felicitate the British government on victory in the great war and at the same time to discuss his father's relations with the British in Arabia. It was an eminently successful visit, and at the same time an initiation—rather a difficult one, we might surmise—into foreign affairs for the young prince.

Whatever else it was, it gave him a taste for travel which has never left him. Some of his early journeys were private, including one to the United States with his young brother Khalid (now Crown Prince); in 1920, and later in official capacities, either as Foreign Minister, representative at the United Nations, or, most recently, as King. In the years 1919–1924 he could consider himself, to some extent anyhow, a private person, and could journey as a sightseer without attracting attention. Those were, of course, only five years, and preceded by a good many years the great wealth of his family, so it is improbable that he spent money very lavishly. Even so, some of those far-off private journeys must have given him impressions more vivid, newer and more enduring than the official visits of later years, for his face lighted up with the reminiscence as he told me about them.

In Arabia itself the old King was at this period expanding his realms quite steadily, and to each new conquest the young prince was sent for experience both military and civil. An Arab prince of such rank—so near to the throne—had to know the country and the tribes as well as the techniques of desert warfare, riding, shooting and falconry. The mountain province of Asir on the Red Sea was annexed by Abd el-Aziz in 1920—it had been technically Turkish but was now in anarchy and welcomed the Sa'udi bringing order—and the Rashidi domains in 1921, Jauf and Wadi Sirhan in 1922. At last, in 1924, came the quick triumph over the Hejaz, followed by a long, almost bloodless siege of Jiddah and the consolidation of the new territories into one country.

In all of this Prince Faisal played a part of growing importance. He distinguished himself not only by military skill and bravery, which were almost taken for granted in his family, but by an ability to deal with strangers which was far less usual. He liked talk, he could argue with the best of them, and he had a natural love of Bedouin poetry which enabled him to enjoy long desert evenings by the fire. To this day, when he quotes Bedouin poetry—some of it has been written down but much is still oral, repeated from region to region and generation to generation—his whole face changes and he seems to think of other scenes, other times. There are a few photographs from his youth which show in the boy of eighteen or nineteen some quality of eagerness for life which does not strike us so much in his brothers or other contemporaries. (Hindsight is common, all too easy to fall into; yet this does seem to me to shine out from the old photographs.)

At this period of his life, before officialdom seized upon him, he was distinguished for riding and shooting, even in the company his father kept; and he had acquired his own particular passion for falconry, which he is said to retain. That is, he no longer has the time he had in his youth (or that his father had) for hunting and shooting; his tasks are far too complicated and arduous, demanding more time than there is; and yet he still likes to count over his falcons and admire the gleam of their wings. Even the horses (and there are some wonderful beauties in the royal stables) do not compel his attention today, but I have heard that the strangely gifted birds, bred for centuries in Arabia, still interest the King.

A youth of such mettle had no trouble accommodating himself to conditions in mountain or seacoast, plain, desert or tribal oasis. He was, it seems, eager to know all the new territories and their peoples, quick to learn their turns of phrase or their dialects, fascinated by local customs, traditions and differences. From an early age (and doubtless the influence of the grandfather can be seen here too) he spoke a clearer, more generally understood Arabic than was common in his family or in Nejd. It was possible for him to be readily understood in Mecca when he first went there as a conqueror at the age of eighteen, which (they tell me) was not the case with his father or brothers. This gift for language, which amounts to a great interest in Faisal's life, has given him his joy in poetry, his esteem for classical Arabic and his pleasure in its literature even of today. In his youth it was one of the things that most distinguished him from his contemporaries and marked him out, all along, as being the member of the family who ought to deal with the foreigners. It was a case of early and immediate adaptation to a hitherto unknown necessity, and his capacity for such an adaptation must have been innate, since it had been shown in him alone, regardless of the common environment.

He was not to have a long period of private life, in or out of Arabia, to pursue his travels or investigations. The old King knew him to have the special qualities we have indicated and in fact made him Viceroy of the Hejaz at the age of nineteen. He took up his residence in Mecca in the governor's palace (to which he has now appointed one of his brothers) but spent much of his time in Jiddah, the port of Arabia—its window on the world—in the same palace, or office building, where he works today. And even today, although the King, court and a good deal of the government centre there, the people of Jiddah call it 'the Viceroy's Lodge' (El Niyaba). It is a Victorian Turkish edifice like a rather overgrown French villa, with a gravelled approach through a walled garden which contains the usual oleander and bougainvillaea. The King's audience chambers and office, on the first floor up from the slightly raised ground floor, are perhaps more sumptuously carpeted than in Turkish days, but everything else looks as if it had been there a long time. Bodyguard and soldiery—indeed, any show of force—are confined to the garden and entrance.

The attraction of Mecca to him from early days has appeared in a number of his speeches then and since: he was drawn to the holiest of Islamic centres by nature as well as doctrine, and has often referred to Mecca as his 'second home', where, in fact, he spent far more time than in Nejd: 'The days I spent in Mecca were the prime of my life and the prime of my youth, that I shall never forget.' (May 29th, 1963.) His studies in Koranic literature and Arab poetry have been pursued in those surroundings which, for centuries past, have drawn the learned and the studious from all parts of Islam: there quite evidently is a special atmosphere in the birthplace of the Prophet, to which Faisal, of all men, is sensitive.

But it was in Jiddah after 1925 that he came most into contact with the foreigners and the Arabs who dealt with them. Mecca, after all, has been a restricted area in modern times and its life depends largely on the annual pilgrimage. Jiddah, as an open port which had traded with the whole world for ages past, is Arabia's gateway to Europe and the Middle East. The Persian Gulf on the other side of the peninsula naturally looked towards India and Iraq rather than to

the west, and since its ports were smaller and mostly not yet developed, it could not play the part which Jiddah and the Red Sea historically had played for the whole region. The young Prince Faisal,
representing his father in this commercial and diplomatic centre, had
to accustom himself to ways of thought and action which were not
those of the central desert, and to a general level of negotiating skills
which must have been, even in the 1920's, above ordinary experience.
He took to it, by all the evidence, as his natural realm, and to this
day his country has had no other Foreign Minister.

It is in the Viceroy's Lodge that Faisal matured and learned to know
the foreign diplomats, the merchants, the financiers and the world.
He never lived there, and from the earliest period he used it as an
office to which his hours of attendance are as punctual and regular as
those of any employee. His own house (not his brother's great unfinished palace which they say he never intends to use, but a smaller
structure of his own doing) is out on the road north to Medina.

Of his private life in these early days as viceroy we know little,
since it is not seemly in Arabia to profess awareness of such things.
He was married in his first youth, by arrangement, no doubt to settle
or appease some tribal matter (a great habit of his father's government); his eldest son, the clever, quick-witted and volatile Prince
Abdullah, is the child of this union. The love of his life, his monogamous Queen, comes a good deal later and we shall try to say what
can be said or learned (in so far as it is possible under the customs) in
the right place. At all events we hear from all sources that Faisal
never took advantage of the polygamy permitted under Islam,
and although his is indeed the modern tendency both in Arabia and
neighbouring countries, princes of wealth and rank seldom have
shown such restraint. (In the Sa'udi family polygamy has been the
rule, even on a scale seldom seen in other Arab countries.) The
modern tendency, perceptible quite early in the nineteenth century
in some countries, has steadily diminished polygamy and other forms
of licence, so that in a good many Arab countries, as well as in Arabia
itself, it has become unusual among ordinary people; this does not
apply to princes; of his own approximate rank, Faisal is said to be
practically unique.

Today there is a big modern building to house the Foreign Office
in Jiddah, and there are, of course, functionaries and files galore.
There is no doubt a precedent for everything, an apposite tradition
and an authority that can be cited. There was little of all this ready to
hand when Faisal took over. The Sharifian regime in the Hejaz had

been eminently personal—Hussein himself attended to most things—
and many transactions were never recorded. The creation of a Foreign
Office, a functioning apparatus for the control of relations with other
countries, although it took about thirty years or more to achieve, was,
like so much else in the country, Faisal's doing: not that he could do it
all himself (or that he even tried), but in the sense that he supplied the
incessant drive and the urge towards coherence which animated the
infant bureaucracy.

The diplomatic and consular representatives of the foreign powers
were accustomed to Jiddah, and Abd el-Aziz wisely decided to let them
stay there. In principle he was not very eager for foreigners to live in
Riyadh—at an earlier stage he had restricted their visits out of
caution, since the Wahhabi were not theoretically friendly to the
infidel; and even until much later the old King expected foreigners
to wear Arab clothing in the Nejdi capital. Mecca, of course, was forbidden to all but Muslims. This left the commercial capital, the port
of Jiddah, as the only one where the foreigner could live and circulate
freely, and the Foreign Office quite naturally came into being on those
terms, and, as it happened, as an adjunct to the viceroy's government.
Later on foreigners went to Riyadh quite freely but the embassies and
consulates, as well as the Arab Foreign Office, remained in Jiddah,
and as a matter of convenience this is likely to be the system for
years to come. Supplies, by and large, come in by sea, and that alone
would be a determining consideration for most of these offices.

I have never settled to my own satisfaction the question of how
much English Faisal learned during this period of his viceroyalty
(say, 1925–1935) and how he went about it. Obviously he knows a
good deal of English. I have been present when he argued with his
interpreters about the meaning of certain English words (how to put
them into Arabic, what they really mean) and there is no question
that his acquaintance with the language is considerable. His present
wife Queen Iffat also speaks French, I have been told, and almost all
the younger princes and princesses have some knowledge of these
languages. (The boys are fluent in English.) Faisal must have learned
gradually and with more difficulty, since his opportunities were more
limited, his time more occupied and since he did not start the study
until after he was twenty, and then, I suppose, not really systematically. Even so, he is seldom at a loss in any international gathering
and, although well served by his interpreters (chief of them the
admirable Sheikh Abd el-Aziz Majid, of Sudanese origin), he has by
no means a total dependence upon them.

84

Those early years in Jiddah—up to, perhaps, 1932 and the proclamation of the kingdom, followed by the Yemen campaign—were no doubt idyllic in many ways, conducive to study and reflection for a thoughtful young prince. In the first place, the peninsula was almost entirely at peace. Not since the days of the Prophet had such unity and order fallen upon the Arabian lands. The severity of the old King's repressions—along with his generosity in gifts—had practically suppressed intertribal warfare and blood feuds. The pilgrims to Mecca were protected as never before and came in ever-increasing numbers. Trade grew with order. There was no wealth in the realm—King Abd el-Aziz was always short of money—but there was a kind of precarious equilibrium obtained by much juggling, borrowing and mysterious accounting: the government survived from year to year, even though the British subsidy had ceased. The necromancer of the finances was Abdullah es-Sulaiman, the old King's famous treasurer who kept the treasury under his bed* Innovation had indeed begun, but not on the scale it has since attained, and the camel was still the principal wealth of the Arab. There must have been a sort of peaceful interlude, a long moment of calm, before the oil discoveries and other novelties almost without number dispelled the stagnation of the centuries for ever.

In this moment of calm, that is, between his eighteenth and his twenty-sixth years, Prince Faisal was able to prepare himself for his destiny, that is, chiefly in Mecca and Jiddah, growing into the roles to which his wise and curiously prescient father had assigned him. He was the King's representative in the most advanced and prosperous part of Arabia; he was also Foreign Minister, in the very beginning of a foreign office which was before long to grow into the first great department of the state, with an incipient civil service and a multitude of duties.

The question of the form and status of the new country now came to the fore and there is no doubt that Faisal had a considerable part in the solution. Obviously it could not go on forever under the name of 'Nejd and its Dependencies', since Nejd itself was such a small and relatively insignificant part of the whole. As a matter of fact it was, by the early 1930's, Arabia—it was, practically speaking, the whole of Arabia except the small British protectorates of the south coast; it was much more nearly the whole of Arabia, of Arabia Felix or Arabia Deserta, the historic unit, than there ever had been in one piece

---

* Impossible, as I have been told, but widely believed.

before. Under such conditions the temptation to call it simply Arabia must have been great, but there were counter-arguments, and in addition the pride of the House of Sa'ud came into it. The decision of 1932 was to proclaim it the Kingdom of Sa'udi Arabia and to send Faisal as its ambassador to all the principal powers of Europe to announce the event. For the first time as an adult (he was twenty-six) he represented his father in foreign capitals and as Foreign Minister. The journey was epochal in Faisal's life; although brief, as such journeys so often are—a few days in each capital—he obtained a sudden kaleidoscopic view of what was to be a dominant interest for much of his life: the world outside Arabia, the great world of international relations and politics.

He even visited Soviet Russia on this tour since Russia was first to recognize Sa'udi Arabia, although the relations between their two countries were virtually non-existent and have so remained. It is true that Russian Muslims come as pilgrims to Mecca every year but their numbers are restricted and they constitute about the only form of intercourse between the two countries. Aside from this, there was a fundamental lack of sympathy for the Russian Revolution in Arabia (as formerly in all Arab countries); the Russians at that period were more inclined to play the Zionist card than any of the various Arab alternatives; it is only in recent years (and chiefly as the result of Gamal Abd el-Nasser's activity) that they have taken much part in Middle Eastern affairs. I have heard from friends of King Faisal, in the past years, opinions which show that the Russian influence in any part of the Middle East is deplored by court circles.

'The worst thing Nasser has done,' one friend said with great candour, 'was to bring Russia into the affairs of the Arab world. It was not necessary and it is a bad thing for everybody concerned.'

These opinions—evidently not shared in Egypt, Syria and Iraq—may not be precisely those of King Faisal but it is difficult to suppose that they differ much. Indeed the court in Arabia seldom does differ from the King, for obvious reasons, and the present attitudes reflect a distrust of Russia which goes deep and comes from far back.

The question is often asked whether a rivalry existed at this period between the Crown Prince Sa'ud, heir to the throne and his brilliant young brother Faisal. From all I can make out, there was no serious falling-out between them in the 1920's and 1930's. They were of quite different tastes, characters, temperaments and ideas; to my way of thinking they do not even resemble each other in appearance; and yet they seem to have pulled together in harness quite amicably most of the time. With Sa'ud governor of Nejd and Faisal viceroy of the Hejaz they were far enough apart to make their meetings infrequent, while Sa'ud's duties in the central desert and with the Bedouin were diverse from Faisal's with diplomacy and foreign affairs. No two brothers (or rather half-brothers) can have been much more different than these two. Sa'ud had charm and generosity, indeed, and at a time when the revenues of the state were not too lavish these qualities were deplored; but he had little liking for the hard work and regularities of steady government; he was profusely polygamous at a time when (in spite of the example given by their father) the institution of plural marriages was declining in Arabia as a whole, while it practically disappeared in neighbouring countries; and, perhaps most of all, the young people growing up simply could not look upon him as an ideal prince or the repository of a future role in their history or that of their country.

These divergences, somewhat between the two princes but even more in the attitudes of others towards them, were to deepen and broaden with the years. There came a time when orderly government was no longer possible with Sa'ud on the throne; but I have no information that would make me think the drama started early. I think, on the contrary, that during the lifetime of the old King there was no such drama, and that it only reached its climax in the grave events of the 1960's.

The old King permitted very little independence of judgment on the part of his sons in matters which he regarded as important. There are famous examples of his sternness. The most famous, in Yemen, came when Prince Faisal (accompanied by the younger Sulaiman, brother of the King's treasurer) led an invasionary force which swiftly conquered the mountain country and was about to occupy Sana, the capital, whereupon an imperious telegram from the old King told them to evacuate the country at once and return to their bases. Prince Faisal on this occasion disregarded his father's wishes and proceeded in his course, until a second telegram of terrible import reached him and made him pause. He and Sulaiman then swiftly obeyed their orders and returned to Sa'udi territory.

It seems, from what I can make out, that the old King was on quite good terms—of comprehension, anyhow—with the Imam Yahia, the old one, and had come to an agreement with him on frontiers. The invasion of the Yemen was ordered because of a border dispute: there seems not the slightest doubt that some errant forces of the Imam had invaded the mountain province of Asir, now for a decade established as Sa'udi territory. It might have been a border raid of the kind common in Arab history but the Sa'udi kingdom, new in its force and pride, was not to be treated so lightly; Faisal as viceroy of the Hejaz then invaded Yemen.

Of this much-discussed episode I have heard many stories, no doubt campfire tales for the most part, embellished and elaborated by the Bedouin imagination. For example, I have heard no less than five versions, as I recall, of the old King's celebrated telegram to Prince Faisal. In one of these versions the spicy language is almost enough to discredit the story (I know if I used such language the telegraph companies would not accept it—but perhaps Kings are different). In another version King Abd el-Aziz is supposed to heave threatened his son with decapitation ('I will have your head') if he did not immediately withdraw from the Yemen.

Such haughty tones were not unknown to King Abd el-Aziz. However, on the one occasion when I spoke of the matter to King Faisal he smiled gently and gave me a much quieter version of the story.

'I was young', he said, 'very young. I did not understand. Military exploits, conquest and all that kind of thing make an appeal to youth. My father was of course completely right, in that he drew the line at aggression. Provocation there was, but to take over a neighbouring country is not right, it is an aggressive thing to do and I realize it now. I recall a Bedouin poem, which I have no doubt rendered very lamely, about the magic of youth. I thought the poem was not far off saying— in essence—something which used to be one of Bernard Shaw's famous remarks, that youth was much too good to be wasted on the young.'

It was altogether a buoyant period of Faisal's life, those years from 1932 to 1934 or 1935, since it brought to him his monogamous and very happy marriage with the Lady Iffat, now Queen. Enquiry into the domestic affairs of the Arab princes is not encouraged (to put it mildly) in Arabia, and I have nothing in particular to report about the Queen, whom I never saw; but there is general agreement among those who know Faisal best that he has been a happy man in his monogamy—far more so than his relatives in their polygamy—and that the Queen has exerted a beneficent influence upon the whole course of development in the past decades in Arabia.

She is the daughter of an Arab dignitary belonging to the House of Sa'ud, and thus a remote cousin of Faisal's, but her mother was Turkish and she grew up in the much freer atmosphere of Istanbul.

At her father's death she and her mother returned to Arabia, under the protection of the King, and before long Prince Faisal had married her in, as we might say, exclusivity. Only those acquainted with the Arabian peninsula could know how rare this is—rare, indeed, to the point of being unique among persons of the highest rank. From the time of their marriage Faisal has been a monogamist.

His preceding marriages had been, in fact, essentially political. The first marriage produced his eldest son, Abdullah, who has now renounced the royal privileges to go into business in Jiddah. By a second marriage which had great significance in tribal politics (to a cousin of the Jiluwi branch of the House of Sa'ud) he had two sons, Khalid and Sa'ud. By his lifelong marriage to the Lady Iffat he has had five sons, Mohammed, Sa'ud, Abd el-Rahman (the one who went to Sandhurst), Bandar and Turki. The eight daughters of the family, although indeed cherished in the family and usually married off to princes of the blood royal, are not considered to be of public concern; their lives are private. I am not able to name them.

There was a time when King Faisal (before being King) had no less than six sons receiving instruction in the United States, as well as the one at the Sandhurst Military Academy in England. They were attracted to Princeton University, perhaps because of its attention to Arabic and Islamic studies; at all events I believe that when there were six at a time (it was in 1960) they were all either at Princeton or at schools near there.

From the little I know I must say that Faisal has maintained a wonderfully natural and easy relationship with his sons. (With his daughters too, I have no doubt, but upon this my information is limited.) The princes have told me how they could argue with their father and often do. They are not afraid of him. They do not understand him. (Two of them have told me so: I say, 'I do not understand your father', and they say, 'Neither do I'.) But they are ready to dispute with him on some of the most delicate problems of internal administration and external politics, and he joins in the argument as if they were all equals. I am told he values the opinions of the young primarily because they are young—they have not the accrustations he has learned to distrust in the old. He can either listen to their arguments or take part in them, as he chooses, and they never hesitate to speak frankly in front of him. If the arguments get too heated, I have been told, it is the Queen who calms them with a word or two of reproof, not Faisal himself. These sessions of talk are those which take place, in recent years, at eleven at night, shortly before the King goes to bed. The boys and girls are generally there in full force, but not the regular officials or ministers—it is a sort of family party, as I understand it.

And the princes have told me that their father used to spend a great deal of time with them. He cannot do so any more—and besides, they are young men now. But he used to have lunch with them every day, which in view of his commitments to internal and external events was quite remarkable, and he saw them at other fixed hours, such as before the evening prayer. Perhaps he has always paid a great deal of attention to what they said. Perhaps it was only paternal affection. Who knows? I myself think that a great deal of Faisal's awareness of the younger world is due to this constant association with his juniors, his sons and daughters, nieces and nephews, who for many years have been welcome in his family quarters at certain hours of every day.

He has also a favourite sister (so like his father!) to whom he pays visits practically every day when he is in Riyadh. (She does not go to Mecca and Jiddah as often as the rest of the court does.) His deference to his uncles is very marked—indeed, I have heard court officials say it is excessive, that respect to the elders should not be exaggerated.

These details are mentioned only to show that the Prince built up for himself a happy family existence long before he became King, and that it continues. The notion that polygamy destroys the family is in itself false, as the experience of a great part of mankind—the greater part—can prove. The notion that the *idea* of polygamy, or even of successive monogamies, might destroy the family is even more false. We find few examples of closer family ties than we find in Arabia. Of this, Faisal's arrangements might serve as a model and although perhaps not according to the tradition of a thousand years ago, still quite close to the general idea and the essential purpose of the Prophet.

The domestic felicity of Faisal as Prince (and as Viceroy of the Hejaz) by no means filled his days up to his accession to the throne. A large part of his mind and life was then, as now, occupied by foreign affairs, of which he has been the only minister—the heart and soul—since the department came into being as an arm of the government. His father, as by instinct, entrusted this vital activity to him retaining an overriding authority in the main lines of it, as he did in everything else. By 1964 (the year of his accession to the throne) Faisal's experience in foreign affairs was easily higher and deeper, broader and more variegated, than that of anybody else in the kingdom. As he once said to me himself, he knew every one of the Arab leaders, that is, in all the countries of the Arab League and beyond, by personal and usually prolonged acquaintance; his knowledge of men in power in both the west and the east was by this time phenomenal. He had made foreign affairs and the principles upon which foreign policy should be based a lifelong study, a familiar contemplation at all times, and it is not surprising (although perhaps a little unjust) that it should be in this respect that he is first considered abroad. Outside Arabia there is only a limited knowledge of what Faisal has done for the women and children of the country, for the schools, roads, hospitals and public works, but it is very widely understood that he has a distinct point of view in foreign affairs, one which would unite the Islam of tradition (the Islam of Mecca) to progress and public welfare, all of it without the admission of ideologies incompatible with the teaching of the Prophet. It is in this realm that Faisal has made his most individual contribution to international politics.

6 Faisal, Foreign Minister

1

THE Balfour Declaration was signed on November 2nd, 1917, in the form of a letter to Lord Rothschild, head of the Zionist Federation in Great Britain. Actually it was the result of conversations between Chaim Weizmann, head of the Zionist Organization in Great Britain (afterwards first President of the State of Israel), and the British Government in general, particularly Lloyd George, not Balfour.

Arthur James Balfour, author of the enigmatic declaration, was in his seventieth year at the time and had, in the course of a long life as a Conservative office-holder and social ornament, seldom met any Jews outside of the most privileged society. He was the fine flower of a race now departed—nephew of the third Lord Salisbury, poet and philosopher and intermittently politician, always the centre of his own world of wits and mutual admirers, 'the Souls', as they were called, with Margot Asquith as another central animator. Mr. Balfour had the supreme knack of forgetting what he wished to forget, and there is a story that he actually did forget why the Balfour Declaration was named after him. (This was in his final years.)

At all events, he signed it. It read as follows:

'My dear Lord Rothschild,
    His Majesty's Government view with favour the establishment in Palestine of a national home for the Jewish people, and will use their best endeavours to facilitate the achievement of this object, it being clearly understood that nothing shall be done which may prejudice the civil and religious rights of existing non-Jewish com-

munities in Palestine, or the rights and political status enjoyed by Jews in any other country.'

No snake could ever have eaten its own tail more successfully than this. 'A national home for the Jewish people' was one thing—not, indeed, what the Zionists wanted: they wanted 'the' national home, implying nation and state—but it was flatly contradicted by the next part of the sentence. Clearly you cannot establish a national home (whether you call it nation or state or not, so long as it implies great immigration) in one country without detriment to the interests of the inhabitants of that country. The Balfour Declaration was self-defeating from the start. If it meant anything at all it meant what it has resulted in—the creation of a Jewish Zionist state in an Arab world, with the remaining Arab population forever condemned to subsidiary status.

How could it have been otherwise?

The response of the Arabs was immediate and has never varied, except in degree, since 1918. The Palestine Arabs in their various revolts (1919, 1929, 1936) have never had enough physical force to impress their will, and the disjointed, haphazard attack by the Arab states on Israel at its formation (1948) was a failure. Triumphant in money, arms and ammunition, the Zionists have imposed a state on the Arab world which arouses the deepest, the most ineradicable opposition in every Arab of whatever school of thought. It is difficult to imagine any circumstances in which this will change.

Now, mind you, the early days of the 'national home' in Palestine were different. The Zionist official leaders never stopped stating in public that they desired no nation or state, only a 'national home' (whatever it might mean). The rebel 'revisionists', headed by Vladimir Jabotinsky, asked for full national sovereignty over a huge area reaching beyond the Jordan, and hinted widely at further conquests. Their programme, disowned by official Zionism in the 1920's and even the 1930's, has become a commonplace of Zionism today. Nobody at the present time could doubt that the ultimate aim of Zionism is an ever-enlarging realm at the expense of the Arab world. No frontiers have been accepted, or will be accepted, for this unstipulated realm. To add to the anomaly, a great spokesman for the State of Israel (Ben Gurion, long Prime Minister) is on record as proclaiming that every Jew in the world, regardless of his status, is a citizen of Israel if he so wishes.

In this extraordinary situation, for which history offers no parallel, it would be strange indeed if the Arabs did not react.

They did so from the start. I have it on King Faisal's word that this was the first awareness he ever had of international politics or what it might mean. I am not clear (and he did not make it clear to me) precisely when his father's court at Riyadh became aware of the Balfour Declaration. He was only eleven or twelve years of age, obviously. Whether the old King heard the news as soon as it was announced, or after some delay, I cannot establish. (There was a delay even in London—indeed the British carried secrecy so far as to misinform their allies, including President Wilson according to his ambassador Page, before the climax.) The political object of the Balfour Declaration as announced at the time was to rally Jewish opinion (and wealth and power), particularly in the United States, to the Allied cause in the war. One might have thought this no longer necessary after the entry of the United States in the war, but these clouded judgments have always dogged the Palestine difficulty.

Faisal tells me he was stricken to the depths by this news of a new and alien state in Arabia. He says it was his first perception of foreign affairs and that he has never to this day recovered from the shock.

We are all victims of hindsight and perhaps the King was not, as a child of eleven, quite so stricken as it now seems to him that he was. At the same time he heard of it constantly from then on and it undoubtedly established a sort of beginning-point, a starting-post, for his life in foreign affairs.

It was, from the beginning, a matter of essential imposture. The British government, whether honourably (through stupidity) or dishonourably (through evil intent) never carried out the Balfour Declaration, nor could any other government have carried it out. To open the gates for floods of alien immigration would be to submerge the existing population, obviously. Only Hitler could do this. The British then tried to moderate the Jewish immigration with equally obvious results—discontent on both sides. The Declaration was the plainest, neatest statement of impossibility that it is possible to imagine in international affairs, and so it worked out, year after year. It was accepted by the international conference at San Remo in 1920 (without Russian agreement) and on July 24th, 1922, the Council of the League of Nations approved a 'mandate', a new and convenient word for colony, by which Great Britain was to govern Palestine in accordance with the terms of the Balfour Declaration. The Declaration was written into the preamble of the mandate.

Over a month earlier, that is on June 3rd, 1922, Winston Churchill as Colonial Secretary had stated in the House of Commons that the

Balfour Declaration did not mean 'imposition of a Jewish nationality upon the inhabitants of Palestine as a whole', and never the 'disappearance or the subordination of the Arabic population, language or culture in Palestine'. That which he declared to be impossible has methodically taken place. Indeed, after a very long time during which the chiefs of Zionism denied any desire for a separate nation or state, the State of Israel was proclaimed on May 14th, 1948, thirty and one-half years after the Balfour Declaration. Within 12 minutes by the White House clocks it was recognized by Mr. Truman, thirty-third President of the United States, personally by telephone to the Associated Press.

These are the thirty years of Faisal's growing up into foreign affairs. It is scarcely surprising that such events and those connected with them have formed his mind in one respect. Like every other Arab, he resents bitterly the formation of the State of Israel at Arab expense, and if there were any chance of eradicating it he would take that chance. He has made it abundantly plain to me that on this question he is inaccessible to compromise.

I cannot and do not speak for the King, but I can say that when I did introduce this subject to him in conversation I received short shrift. I asked him if he could foresee any possible conversation or accommodation with the State of Israel. He replied: 'None which is compatible with the existence of that State.' That was enough for me. I never tried again.

Of course this is the merest commonplace among Arabs. They murmur it in their sleep. And yet most of them do not really mean it as Faisal does. He lived through it, spiritually speaking, as very few of the other Arab leaders have, because he is not selfish. They have lived through it for their selfish reasons but he only because in his deepest regions, his absolute faith, he is outraged by Zionism.

It is, indeed, hard to explain to western minds, but the notion of a Zionist state in the middle of the Arab world is offensive to all Arabs and, further, to all Islamic peoples. Mecca, Jerusalem, Damascus, Medina—these cities of the desert are dear to the peoples of the desert, holy in some senses, and above all Mecca, holiest of all. The idea of a modern western state, militarized to the highest degree— where every man, woman and child is taught to bear arms—thrust into the middle of this desert, with easy access to any part of it, turns the Arab mind to fury. I have not yet seen nor do I expect soon to see any abatement of this fury. The Zionists, with their modern equipment, may thrust equally at Damascus or at Mecca, and with temporary successes—brilliant triumphs—but the strong chance of ultimate destruction. This is the sinister checkmate in the desert.

Faisal knows all this better than almost anybody. The tribes are his: anybody who has seen him with the tribes, even the tribes of Africa, knows that he is their prince and king. The pseudo-modern attempts of Nasser in Egypt and other leaders elsewhere do not affect Faisal's effect upon the Arabs and even (I have been told) the non-Arab tribes, as in Persia.

Now, as it happens, this is common enough. I doubt if anybody could survive long in an Arab community if he advocated an accommodation with Israel. Habib Bourguiba, who once made a very tentative offer in that direction (one which Israel would never have accepted) was branded as a traitor in many Arab states for even suggesting it. Of course Israel cannot have peace—and does not want peace—so long as it will not agree to a frontier. Of course Arabia is at war so long as there is no frontier. The events of 1967 must prove this if nothing else.

Faisal is the one Arab prince who is both involved and not involved. He is vowed to oppose the State of Israel, but he also has no frontiers with that state and no direct conflict with it, day by day, as have Egypt, Syria and Jordan. He is in that sense above the battle, although his heart is deeply concerned in it. He realizes that this is one way in which the Arab world is profoundly at one, even though it may not know what to do about it.

And why not?

Obviously the United States stands as the protector of the State of Israel, although a nationwide American plebiscite would probably reject such an assumption. The relatively small Jewish vote in the United States—formerly merged in the general vote, but now substantially Zionist—is vital in New York, Philadelphia, Boston, Los Angeles and Chicago. This could elect a president.

Faisal has understood this for quite a few years, since his first interview with Roosevelt. He has also understood that the full power of the United States can and would be used for the protection of the State of Israel if the necessity occurred. Against the power of the United States there is at present nothing to avail.

2

Across this fundamental anti-Zionist policy, which has its depths in Faisal's religious loyalty, there is cut another policy almost as deep, which is the resistance to domination by Egypt.

Egypt (which for a long time meant the Turks) claimed and exercised authority over various parts of Arabia at various times. No population figures are dependable for these countries but it seems fairly safe to say that Egypt has over thirty million inhabitants while Arabia has something between three and six millions. This is an enormous difference. It is made more striking when we reflect that the true *per capita* income (difficult or impossible to estimate) is much higher in Arabia than in Egypt. The wealth of Egypt, dependent mainly upon cotton, fluctuates wildly every year, whereas the wealth of Arabia, dependent upon an almost inexhaustible supply of petroleum, goes up all the time. The Egyptian superiority in tradition, culture, architecture and historical unity has been steadily whittled away by the present century, and although it may be true that Egyptian architects dominate the new landscape of the desert (the 'New Towns', as they say in England), it is also true that the prestige of everything Egyptian has steadily declined, along with the current Arab notion of Egyptian friendship.*

It could scarcely be otherwise since the regime of Gamal Abd el-Nasser set as its constant aim the opposition to Sa'udi Arabia in every realm, socially, politically and economically. It would obviously be a tremendous advantage to an impoverished Egypt (whatever its claim to historical superiority in Islam) to have the resources of Arabia— and along with Arabia itself, that is Sa'udi Arabia, those of the tiny Persian Gulf states of startling wealth, and the wealth that may come from the southern sheikhdoms, and, perhaps ripest for the plucking, the vast income of the Kuwait sheikhdom at the head of the Persian Gulf. These stupendous revenues as they stand today would change

---

* Since the Six-Day War of June, 1967, between the State of Israel and its immediate Arab neighbours, much has changed. Sa'udi Arabia, along with Kuwait and Libya, now subsidizes Egypt at an enormous rate 'until the Suez Canal shall be re-opened'. Arabia pays fifty million pounds sterling each year to Egypt and Jordan, the principal sufferers from the Israeli war (thirty-seven to Egypt and thirteen to Jordan). These fifty million pounds—offered by King Faisal at the Khartoum conference after the war—have now become fifty-seven million pounds, owing to the devaluation of that currency. Kuwait is paying fifty-five millions sterling and Libya thirty millions each year. These countries, all of them enriched by regular oil royalties from the west, are in this way compensating the sufferers for an inability, largely geographical, to come to their aid in time. The Six-Day War enlarged the State of Israel to six times its previous size, at the expense of the Arab neighbours, and closed the Suez Canal to the world's traffic. King Faisal has wished, and his fellow-sovereigns in Kuwait and Libya have concurred in this, to make up the losses (or some of them). Actually I suppose that the dictatorship of Gamal Abd el-Nasser never had so much cash in hand at any one time before.

the entire state of affairs in the Middle East—or, if the term is pre-ferred, in West Asia. The existing arrangements between the various oil companies and the governments now in power would be enough for Egypt: with such dollar and pound resources the Egyptian government could flourish exceedingly for years to come, until it became advisable (sooner or later) to nationalize the properties themselves.

All this is fairly obvious. What is less obvious is the persistence of the Egyptian government in pursuing its aim, now in this way and now in that, so that Sa'udi Arabia may be isolated and eventually overcome.

As we have seen earlier, the dynasty of Mohammed Ali (that is, Albanians who had become Turks) was quite clear in aim at the Arabian peninsula, and it was only the jealous animosities of the European powers that prevented an Egyptian conquest in the nine-teenth century. The purpose of empire in that case was a little com-plex: it had to do with control of the Islamic holy places, Mecca and Medina above all, and of the military manpower of the Arab tribes, along with considerations of grandeur and prestige. Material con-siderations, at least on the enormous scale known to us at the present time, did not weigh much: the wealth of the desert was still unknown. But there remains a memory in the desert tribes of the conflict of the past century and to a lesser degree it remained in Egypt too—as of an unfinished battle, a dispute still to be resolved.

This ancestral memory is as nothing, of course, compared to the active longing aroused in Egypt at the present time by the revenues of the Arab states with Sa'udi Arabia at their head. From the point of view taken by Gamal Abd el-Nasser the Arab states are of right one country and ought to be one country (one could even agree with him so far) except that he always thought this one country should be led by Egypt with himself as absolute dictator. It is here, as well as in the desire to acquire enormous assets belonging to others, that Nasser most alienated the intellectuals and the youth of the Arab world. They were willing to acquiesce in his courtship of the Soviet Union, and they were wildly enthusiastic when he defied the combined powers of the West (Suez was his highest point). When it comes to dictatorship he ran against a division of opinion which, so far as I can tell or estimate, might have brought his career to a close even before his death in September, 1970.

Just now I said that the intellectuals and youth were willing to acquiesce in his courtship of the Soviet Union, but even here I must qualify. I have heard young intellectuals say that his introduction of the Soviet Union into the affairs of the Arab world has been a disaster, that it can only disrupt and destroy those whom it seeks to aid, and that if there is ever a civil war among Arabs it will be because of this policy.

Faisal himself clearly shares this point of view. He has not been sparing in his denunciation of 'subversive' influences and 'alien' ideologies, but these often wear (in neighbouring countries, that is) a very Arab guise. If I were to guess at his wariness of Nasser it would be first of all a guess at his concern for the security of his realm. I think he wants to preserve his dynasty just as all kings wish to preserve their dynasties: I think he wants to keep Arabia intact as he received it; and I believe he feels a deep threat to the security and to the territorial integrity of his country in many of Nasser's activities. This, of course, comes to a head in the civil war in the Yemen.

The Yemen, a country of wild mountains and many children, is in a way the origin of the Arab world, culture and language. T. E. Lawrence once described the Arab migrations to the north as 'a human Gulf stream' pouring out of the Yemen across the desert in search of fertility—the 'Fertile Crescent', we say now. Something of this kind undoubtedly did take place, long ago, leaving tribes in the desert along the way, eventually Arabizing the whole of Syria, Lebanon, Palestine, Iraq and segments of countries beyond. This was long before the Prophet—it was in some period which has not been dated with any accuracy, and as we have already seen, in the Prophet's time most of these dwellers in the Fertile Crescent were Christians, as they had been for centuries. It was the Prophet's teaching (and the tyranny of the Greeks) that turned them to Islam.

Yemen as the source of the Arab flood has not interested the world conquerors up to recent years. We do not know that even Napoleon, that assiduous searcher after likely bits, had hit upon it in his scheme for the Red Sea approach to India. We know that the Turks, in their rather desultory and half-hearted way, claimed it before 1914 and shed no tears when it was (quite easily) wrested from them at the end of the first world war. The Imam who came to power, Yahia, was a friend of old Abd el-Aziz and they understood each other very well. It was only the slight flurry of 1932–1933, when Faisal invaded the mountain country, that clouded this relationship. In subsequent years there was no dispute between Sa'udi Arabia and the Yemenite monarch, although the latter had (even before Yahia's death) engaged the Russians to do some work on ports and roads.

99

The Russians were, in fact, well engaged in their useful endeavours in that country before Gamal Abd el-Nasser turned his eyes in that direction. Perhaps they encouraged him to do so? Who is to tell? I have heard from American political officers that there was one moment (I date it 1960, early summer) when the Russians, Americans and Chinese were all busily engaged building roads for the Yemenites. I am sure these roads, if not altogether in ruins, have served for the transport of Egyptian tanks and motor transport, as well as artillery, from the coast to the capital.

Faisal was in a period of temporary eclipse when the open Egyptian invasion of Yemen took place (September, 1962). He was in New York, representing his brother King Sa'ud at the United Nations, and not in control of the royal government at home. He did, however, take advantage of a luncheon at the White House to warn the president, Mr. J. F. Kennedy, against recognition of the 'republic' of the Yemen, which would, he said, prove to be an Egyptian puppet government. Mr. Kennedy disregarded this warning in January, 1962, by recognizing the 'republic' of the Yemen, whose principal members were executed by the Egyptians two years later.

There would be little profit in pursuing the story of the civil war in the Yemen from 1962 to now. It has been the story of outright invasion by the Egyptian army in support of a regime which it has now partly rejected. On the other side the Sa'udi government (since 1964, Faisal) resolutely supported the forces of the young Imam, the so-called 'royalists'. As Faisal remarked to me rather sourly two or three years ago, these are western terms corresponding to no local reality. In fact the opposing forces are the Egyptian invaders and the Yemenite defenders who are supported by arms and munitions from Arabia. In other words, it is the old opposition of the Egyptian and the Arab. Egypt has found that its 'republicans' were, for varying reasons (mostly plain patriotism) wavering in their support of the invaders. Thus no less than six of the leading ministers of the 'Yemen Republic' were executed by the Egyptian army in 1966.

The amount of double-talk involved in all this surpasses belief. At one point President Gamal Abd el-Nasser of Egypt visited the King of Arabia in state (August, 1965) in a battleship at Jiddah and signed a solemn agreement for the pacification of Yemen by compromise. Ten days later he was in Moscow signing an opposite agreement. He obviously expected King Faisal to perform some imprudent act which would bring about a state of open war between Sa'udi Arabia and Egypt not only in the Yemen (where, on a limited scale it already existed until 1967) but on the entire range of conflict between the two states in South Arabia and the Persian Gulf. Many astute observers doubted that Nasser would push things so far or that Faisal would fall into any of the proffered traps. There are disadvantages to all-out war, chiefly the range of territory open to attack and the fact that the numerical superiority of the Egyptians, although unquestionable, is clouded by many doubts over efficiency, supply and command. The Egyptians have done remarkably badly in three conflicts with Israel, and there is no assurance that they would do better against the Sa'udi. Nor did they by any means distinguish themselves during their five years in the Yemen. For the number of regular troops that they had had in Yemen (a number fixed at seventy-five thousand by their own admission at the maximum) it is incomprehensible that they were not able to bring the 'civil' conflict to the victorious end they desired. When, as a result of the Israeli attack upon them in June, 1967, they were forced to withdraw their forces from the Yemen, they left a 'republican' regime which was not at all what they had had in mind when they invaded that country, and which had many elements of what the western press calls 'royalist' (i.e., tribal adherents to the imamate). At the present moment one cannot truly say who won in the five year war in the Yemen. At his death one can say that Gamal lost. As base for the conquest of the South Arabian coast and the Persian Gulf it is no longer his. His Russian friends might have it within their power to change all this, too, but I somehow doubt if they would care to risk their own lives in such a cause.

The British have evacuated the protectorates of the south coast. This was their declared intention for years past and they have kept their word. (1968 was the date for Aden.) The terrorist organizations, originally organized and supported from Cairo, have faded up into officialdom since 'freedom' descended, and at the last word from Aden (which can be so quickly superseded) there is a military dictatorship. In that part of the world 'military' means any man who has been able to beg, borrow or steal a lethal weapon.

The Americans have never wanted the British to get out of the Persian Gulf, Arabian Sea or Indian Ocean, inconvenient waters for our navy, and it is difficult to suppose that the Americans ever will be willing to take their place. There is thus a tremendous vacuum. King Faisal and the Shah of Persia have understood all this and are struggling to avert catastrophe, but the elements are mixed, mixed indeed, and it would be a rash beholder who dared predict the consequences.

3

In addition to the naked power motives concerned with oil, money and territory, there is one more reason why King Faisal's foreign policy has run counter to that of Egypt and its allies. Never can it be too often or too strongly stated that Faisal believes in the essential truth of Islam under all forms and that he regards the intrusion of Russian ideas or ideology into the Islamic countries as a disaster. He tends, along with his closest advisers, to see Nasser as the man who introduced the Soviet Union into Arab affairs, arming some nations with tanks and aeroplanes, others with a Communist and near-Communist party structure which deflects the course of governments and sometimes overthrows them. Faisal thinks, unless I am greatly mistaken, that the Communistically inclined parties of Syria and Iraq (*communisants* as they are called in the French of the region) are fundamentally opposed to the faith of Islam and would overthrow it if opportunity offered. The unbridled language of the Left press and politicans in those countries, who label Faisal as a 'reactionary' and a 'slave of American imperialism', does nothing to calm down the acrimony. Faisal's opposition is directed as much against what *might be* as against what *is,* and the chances are that even this would be less clear if it were not accompanied by military considerations.

For the Soviet armament of Egypt and Syria is by no means an insignificant matter. Faisal's efforts to counteract it (from English and American sources as a rule, although there are French negotiations also) have been on a more reduced scale. In this extremely complicated situation the state of Israel, which gets arms from many sources, must never be forgotten, since it lies athwart the conflicting aims of Egypt and Arabia, seeking to profit wherever possible.

King Faisal's foreign policy has been, I think, influenced by these three things I have named: First, an implacable aversion to the state of Israel as an invasion of Arab soil; second, a deep political opposition to any Egyptian domination of the Arab world and above all to any Egyptian intrusion into the Arabian peninsula; third, a desire to defend Islam, the Faith of the Prophet, against not only those who might assail it from foreign realms but from those kindred souls, those brothers in the Faith, who might be led astray in neighbouring lands (as in Syria, Iraq and Egypt).

These seem to me the main lines of King Faisal's policy as foreign minister since the beginning—not just lately. In larger, more general terms, he would of course be anti-imperialist, pro-Asian, pro-African

The Ras Tanura refinery, showing the tank farm in the background. This is only a part of the Aramco complex, one of the world's largest and most modern oil refineries.

(above) *Prince Faisal now King Faisal with Sheikh Hafiz Wahba at the United Nations Organisation Assembly at the Central Hall, Westminster, in 1946; this was one of the King's many visits overseas.*

(below) *Members of the Council of Ministers meet with the King. The administration of the Kingdom has changed immeasurably since the days of King Abd el-Aziz.*

The King reads a petition from one of his subjects. In spite of the great demand on his time, Faisal is accessible to anyone who wishes to see him, thus bringing to life a relationship seldom found elsewhere in modern times.

The King and his guests at lunch in the Dwan. This is the first time this scene has been photographed. The table is always laid for about 60 guests and no one is barred from eating at the King's table.

On his visit to England in 1967, King Faisal escorts Queen Elizabeth II into a London hotel where he was host at a banquet in her honour.

(above) *A modern view of Riyadh, capital of Saudi Arabia. Times have changed since King Abd el-Aziz had to strengthen the walls of the city to keep enemies out.*

(below) *A recent extension to the Great Mosque al-Haram at Mecca, the city which welcomes hundreds of thousands of pilgrims every year from all corners of the world.*

Jiddah, the modern commercial centre of Saudi Arabia, a thriving and bustling city-port.

(below) The King speaks to the people—the traditional robes and 20th century radio all blend easily with King Faisal and are a symbol of his country's blending of traditional past and thriving present.

The International Airport at Dhahran, a monument to Saudi Arabia's progress into a land of prosperity, but one in which the old values of Islam are still revered.

and anti-South African. The degree of warmth shown on each point depends upon the situation. For example, Sa'udi Arabia has been anti-French at times and pro-French at other times, depending upon the various attitudes of French governments. Anti-American and anti-British positions at the United Nations have depended upon the generally imperial, non-imperial or anti-imperial attitude of the countries involved. So far as the Americans are concerned Faisal is so far from being their 'slave', as the Moscow line suggests, that he does in fact rap them over the knuckles quite often and with salutary results. The Americans are by no means so stupid as to think that because they are making money out of Sa'udi Arabia this gives them special privilege—on the contrary, they do everything in their power to do honour to the King and to respect his wishes. The oil companies are particularly assiduous in this regard, and the Sa'udi government, which in fact has nothing to do with the work of the oil companies (as foreigners seldom understand), nevertheless goes its limit to be comprehending.

One must be quite explicit: true capitalism has ceased to exist except in the United States. It *does* exist there. Private capital on a colossal scale is involved in the oil developments of Arabia. The U.S. government is naturally concerned because millions of Americans are concerned. Taking it to an extreme you might say that the standard of living of the American people is partly dependent upon the oil of Arabia, because the wealth therefrom spreads out into the American community.

This, however, is quite different from a direct government interest in the enterprise. It is unique. The British, French and other democratic governments take as a rule 51 or 52 per cent of the stock of an oil company in order to ensure control. The United States government, alone in the world, has no share in any oil company or any other private company. She remains the one and only monument of private capital.

What we may need here is a reminder of what King Faisal is doing in foreign policy. I will repeat it. He is (1) in unchangeable opposition to the state of Israel; (2) absolutely opposed to any Egyptian claim to control the Arabian peninsula or any part of it; (3) inimical to any political or ideological currents which threaten the Faith of Islam or its broad, essential programme for mankind.

It is in this third aspect of his foreign policy that he has been moved to undertake all those journeys throughout the Islamic world which have constituted the special character of his reign. He has wanted to

E   103

see the countries of Islam and to let them see him, not merely as the sovereign of an Arab state but as the Custodian of the Holy Places of their faith. It is as such, mainly, that he has been received. I have received descriptions of his reception in Persia, for example (spring, 1965) which are very extraordinary in view of the religious differences between that country and his own. He was received as the representative of the Holy Places, and in one sense (emphasized by several witnesses) as a representative of the Prophet Mohammed. It was a spontaneous outburst; no government could have 'arranged' it. And it came from people who were, from the strict Wahhabi point of view, heretics or sectarians.

Similar things happened in Jordan, of course, which is contiguous territory with Sa'udi Arabia and inhabited by many of the same tribes. But the popular enthusiasm in the Sudan (1966) was of the same uproarious character although the racial, geographical and historical differences are deep. I was in the Sudan for the King's visit and witnessed that extraordinary outpouring of Islamic enthusiasm for his person and the idea of his visit—the pilgrimage of the pilgrim, as one may call it.

Faisal has no fanaticism in his character, as he has proved many times over—perhaps most of all in his visit to Persia. In his great farewell speech in the Sudan he welcomed *all monetheisms* to the struggle he perceived between the destructive and constructive elements in the Islamic world. In these visits, without exception up to now, he has stated his willingness to co-operate with all forces of progress which do not aim at the destruction of the Faith. It is implicit, sometimes explicit, that he regards Russian Communism as the enemy of the Faith. Without saying so in as many words, he has made the entire Islamic world-soul, down into Africa itself and across Asia, aware of this opposition which he feels to be profound and ineradicable.

Thus the King's foreign policy, often treated as enigmatic or whimsical, seems on a broad view to be as plain and logical as any known to our century. He would like if there were any possibility of doing so to unite the Islamic nations in an awareness of their common aims and destiny, including an opposition to the innovations or subversive teachings which come from Communist sources.

How many 'innovations'? How many 'subversive teachings'?

One cannot positively tell with King Faisal, although as a rule he tends to make the more trivial things subsidiary to the great questions. In simple matters such as the veiling of women—sumptuary legislation, although symbolical—he does not have a fixed rule. The wives of Sa'udi diplomats in foreign countries are not veiled. The women of his own household discard the veil in foreign countries. And in foreign countries the King is constantly obliged to converse with unveiled ladies, and so far as one has heard, with equanimity. This is true also in Muslim countries, of course. No country except Arabia puts that black tent on their women any more.

What we do not know is the balance King Faisal makes in his mind between historical necessity and present necessity. Of course the women of Arabia must be set free, like other women elsewhere, but when and how? This is the balance he has to settle in his own mind.

Suffering is caused—has been caused—by the modernization of those who are not ready for it. Mustafa Kemal Pasha unveiled the women of Turkey by police power in the 1920's and brought about many sad scenes. In 1927 the armies of the Kuomintang, sweeping across China from the south to the north, forcibly unbound the feet of the Chinese women. It was all right to cut off the pigtail of the man (although it may have been a humiliation for him) but to unbind the feet of women who had been tightly bound since babyhood was a cruel ordeal. It may be true, from all I have heard, that practically every woman in Arabia longs for freedom, at least for freedom from the veil, but there still would be those few minor remnants who would bitterly deplore it.

Faisal has to bear all these things in mind, since he is King of all his people, not some of them. The suddenness of the social revolution also must make him cautious, as well as the enormous difference between points of view in the cities and points of view in the small tribal centres. He had to use troops to open a girls' school in Buraida not long ago (1960), whereas the veiled women of the cities are eager for the sunlight, and in the Bedouin tribes there has never been any real veiling of the women except (in the case of great chiefs) for symbolical reasons. It is a strange triplex situation and the King has so far dealt with it in a manner to conciliate the conservatives although opening education to girls and women.

In respect to travel into or out of the Sa'udi Arabian kingdom it seems to me that on balance the King has been more liberal than his so-called 'Left' neighbours. There was a time, not so long ago either, when it was almost impossible for western journalistic visitors to enter the kingdom; the old King had been misquoted once and denied all visas to those who might do so again. There were fairly severe restrictions on the visa even for Muslim visitors from neighbouring

Muslim states. An enormous number of jobs opened up to the neighbouring Muslims during the 1950's, and there was an influx from Syria, Iraq, Lebanon and Egypt of persons qualified to fill these jobs—school-teachers or clerks, customs officers or post-office officials; the jobs were filled and Sa'udi Arabia today contains many people from neighbouring lands.

The same is not true in reverse. I am told that it is next to impossible for a Sa'udi citizen to go to Baghdad, for example, unless he has certified employment, sponsors, etc., etc. It is not much simpler for Damascus. The idea of just walking down to the airport and buying a ticket is ridiculed amongst those who know the ropes. To go from Sa'udi Arabia to the so-called 'Left' republics of Arabia is by no means easy, even if there be a good reason for going.

No doubt the most conspicuous external sign of Faisal's foreign policy in these years since he became King in his series of journeys abroad, to sympathetic or like-minded Islamic rulers and governments. There were some rather wild stories of a 'Muslim League' or 'Muslim Alliance' as a result of the first few of these visits, but that particular alarm has died down in the face of a cool denial on all sides. These state visits, always calling forth a tremendous popular response, have been to Persia, Jordan, Sudan, Pakistan, Turkey, Morocco, Guinea, Mali and Tunisia, which are by no means of the same political complexion. Persia and Jordan, the first countries visited, are governed by constitutional monarchies; Pakistan was at that time a military dictatorship, Sudan a parliamentary democracy under a republic; Morocco is a constitutional monarchy again, but Guinea and Togo are republics which have been reputed to have a strong 'leftish' tinge. Tunisia is *sui generis* with a constitutional republican government strongly under the control of one man, Habib Bourguiba. The variety of political opinions represented by the rulers of all these states is very wide, and yet the testimony is that King Faisal did well in all of them, arousing the friendship of the politicians and the enthusiasm of the multitude.

My own reason for thinking this soundly based is that in Islam, actually, no King of Arabia, no Keeper of the Holy Cities, could ever be regarded as foreign. If I may put it into terms which may be (perhaps) influenced by Indian ideas, I should say that the thousands who parade and cheer for Faisal in all these countries are influenced by the idea of Mecca—that even if they cannot themselves go to Mecca, Mecca has in this case come to them, so that they receive, somehow or other, some part of the benediction of the holy places.

Faisal carries Mecca with him. It is something like that—although I fully realize how unorthodox any such notions must be from the strict Islamic point of view. However, I have learned that the religious consciousness follows its own laws in all times and places, and orthodox dogma has little to do with its evolution.

The only one of Faisal's journeys of which I have personal knowledge is his visit to the Sudan in the spring of 1966. (March 4th–13th, 1966). I travelled to Khartoum in advance, by commercial airline, so as to be there in the streets on the morning of his arrival. Our flight was delayed and the formalities at the airport were endless, so that I had little sleep indeed before I was out in the streets again to see the King come in.

I was staying at the Khartoum Hotel, on the Blue Nile (it is an annex to the Grand Hotel, and both belong to the railroad monopoly), and there was never any trouble getting into the centre of the city by taxi. I was in the crowd waiting for the King for at least an hour and a half before he, in the company of the President of Sudan, prime minister and other officials drove through. I had plenty of time to observe the behaviour of the crowd—gay, happy, expecting. They were mostly men, as you could expect in a Muslim country, but there were plenty of women and children in the crowd too—the women unveiled, as is usual in the Sudan, or only sketchily veiled by drawing the headscarf over the lower part of the face. It was a good-humoured crowd in spite of intense heat and the long wait, and quite a few people spoke to me during the time—there were few foreigners, western foreigners that is, to be seen in the crowd, and no doubt this aroused some curiosity. I found my interlocutors various enough—one was a merchant with excellent English, some were students who spoke less fluently, but all spoke to me in English. I suppose this was natural courtesy—they could probably tell by looking at me that I could not speak Arabic and they only made remarks when they could do so in my own language. They were friendly, good-tempered, suggesting that I move into a shaded doorway or stand under a tree, etc., etc. It was like a cheerful crowd in India or anywhere else, enjoying a few hours' holiday in order to get a little variety in life—what in India is called *tamasa,* an untranslatable word meaning more or less the excitement (and consequently pleasure) of the crowd gathering.

This was, when the parade finally came along, an enthusiastic crowd, and a thick one too, crowded to the edge of the police lines to see their own President with the Arab King. Great, lusty cheers pierced the hot morning air, and the young boys raced along behind the police lines, as is their custom everywhere, to try to keep up with the King's motor. I should have said it was as warm a welcome as any visitor could desire, and was astonished to find that the Egyptian press of the next day described it as 'cool' or 'lukewarm'. You could not have introduced more people into the main street leading to the palace, nor could they have shown their approval more noisily than they did.

The truth was, of course, that Gamal Abd el-Nasser disliked this most of all King Faisal's visits because it was to his close neighbour the Sudan, to which there can be no doubt Egyptian nationalism still nourishes an ill-founded claim. To minimize the effect of Faisal's visit or even of the hospitality which he received was an obvious device of Nasser's Egyptian journalism, palace-driven and indifferent to objective truth.

During the next few days there were events which showed an extreme devotion to the Arab King from Mecca. I have already said I do not think it was personal—it was for the Keeper of the Holy Cities—and in one sense it was for Mecca, but it reached extraordinary heights outside Khartoum, especially on the Island of Abba, in the White Nile, and at the oasis of Darfur in the western desert.

Abba is the island in the Nile where the Mahdi (the Expected One) retired for contemplation in the years of the 1870's just before his mission began. He was there visited by his Khalifa, who more or less announced or confirmed the mission, and after a certain number of followers had gathered to him, the Egyptians launched an expedition against him by gunboat which landed on the island and was repelled with severe loss. After this victory the volunteers flocked to the Mahdi's standard and his mission, leading to the capture of Khartoum, began in earnest. He was liberating the Sudan, of course, and his was a truly national movement (as Winston Churchill fully recognized in his book on the subject, *The River War*), but he was liberating his country not from the British, who scarcely counted there, but from the Egyptians—known to the Sudan Arabs as 'Turks'. Against these Turks he was successful from beginning to end, until the Gladstone cabinet made the incomprehensible decision to send out 'Chinese' Gordon, a hero of many campaigns, to 'pacify' the country by the mere magic of his name and charm. It was madness, really, since Gordon had no troops and the country was immense—as immense then as today, and much more so. The end was inevitable in the capture of Kartoum and Omdurman, the city across the river (or over the bridge from the confluence of the White and Blue

Niles). The fate of Gordon was followed in a year by the sudden death of the Mahdi himself and the subsequent long rule of his Khalifa or substitute, ending with Kitchener's expedition (1896–1898) in which Churchill fought as a subaltern. That whole epic was rendered vivid by many episodes during those few days, since the nationalist apex reached in 1881 with the Mahdi's revolt and with the Khalifa's rule even afterwards was in a sense the creation of Sudan, as a nation.

On our visit to Abba Island the enthusiasm of the inhabitants reached great heights. From the airport to the government house which was our destination the road was lined with sacrifices (camels and goats) who would, of course, have been sacrificed anyhow (they are always eaten afterwards) but which served to show the determination of the inhabitants to welcome the guest. The dust was beyond belief; we all arrived half-choked and caked in dirt; but there was something about that welcome which surpassed all others. Going away from the ceremonial headquarters to the airfield (after various impressive ceremonies including a mock battle in which the Arabs repelled the 'Turks' and drove them back to their ship) chance willed it that I was in a car with the young Sayyed Saddiq, great-grandson of the Mahdi—very often called 'the young Mahdi' in Sudan—who became prime minister at thirty. Never have I seen anything like the joyous ferocity with which the young leader's followers surrounded that car, risking their lives constantly for a touch of his hand. He was leaning out of the door of the car, extending both arms, touching as many as he could, but the car had to keep going because we were part of a procession and besides the aeroplanes were waiting for us. The pressure stopped us again and again, and Sayyed Saddiq shouted good-natured greetings to the crowds. It was something I have not seen equalled even in India, where the behaviour of crowds so often resembles some weird force of nature, something like a storm at sea.

Afterwards I had a long conversation with Sayyed Saddiq who told me some of what I have already expressed—that enthusiasm for Faisal was not for a foreign visitor; the Sudanese Arabs do not consider Faisal to be a foreigner; his association is with Mecca, which, after all, is only across the Red Sea and where every Arab hopes to go some day. The one-ness of the Arab world was expressed very finely by this remarkable young leader, who was even then waiting for his thirtieth birthday so that he could, constitutionally, be elected to parliament. Once in parliament he could become prime minister whenever he wished, because his party had the majority already. He became thirty soon afterwards, was elected to parliament in a convenient by-election, and became prime minister on July 27th, 1966. It was a wonderful advantage to hear from this gifted young man, in the purest and most expressive English, a view of the future of the Arabs, Arabism and Arabia. It may not have been altogether that prevalent in Faisal's entourage, nor yet in that of Gamal Abd el-Nasser, but it was refreshing that an independent view should be held —and that, too, by the direct descendant of the Mahdi.

Another of our exhibitions in the Sudan was the visit to Nyala, in Darfur, on March 12th, our last day in Sudan. Darfur had once been an independent sultanate in the western (that is, Sudanese western) desert and was famous for its camels and horses, as well as for a breed of warriors who fought on against the British long after the rest of the country was pacified. The President of the Sudan and other great dignitaries, including the highest army officials, went along on these journeys and took care of the arrangements, which seemed to me, in view of all the difficulties of climate and terrain, highly efficient. It was hardly possible to keep to any schedule because on every day of the visit too many things had to be crowded in: one was hardly aware of the horsemanship exhibits (a sort of gymkhana) when it became necessary to go to lunch, and the great parade of camels, thousands upon thousands of camels, was no more than one-third through when we had to go to see the horsemanship. It was always like that because too much had been planned. Fortunately it did not depend on King Faisal to cut short anything which had been arranged in his honour. The President of Sudan simply rose in his place and said there was no more time, that the schedule must go on, that the King appreciated everything but had to get through the programme and get back to Khartoum before nightfall. (There was a state dinner that night at the palace.)

But Darfur with those countless thousands of camels was something nobody who saw it will forget. I have heard that there were fifty thousand camels parading past us, organized by the tribes, and I have heard that there were another fifty thousand still waiting on the vast plain afar off, to take their turn in the parade, after we had been obliged to leave. I even heard some larger figures than these mentioned. All I know is that it seemed like all the camels in the world, many accompanied by their young and with a whole-hearted absence of regular formation which must have delighted a camel's heart. We had horses galore, too, also accompanied by their young and grouped by the tribes, and sometimes the young tribesmen were encouraged to caracole and do tricks, although mostly they trotted past the royal enclosure briskly and without undue display. It was not, therefore, a *fantasia*—there were few of those rousing tricks which go into a *fantasia*—but a parade of camels (and horses, but chiefly camels) such as I have never seen. The heat and dust were forgotten in the extra-ordinary spectacle.

And incidentally, for what it may indicate, I never saw any sign of real fatigue on the part of the King during these celebrations. He looked tired occasionally, as he does in his own palace, and the dust did not spare him any more than it did the rest of us, but of real fatigue, inability to go on, there was no sign. I have noticed before that the presence of great crowds of cheering people has a galvanic effect on public persons, who may—when the day is done and the bath is poured and the bed beckons—feel utterly exhausted, but who, while the mob cheers and the band plays, are equal to any required appearance. (I saw it in India when I travelled with Nehru—he was vibrant with youth until the day's end, when he crumpled with fatigue.) The demands made upon such persons are endless, ruthless and unavoidable. I was myself often shattered by a full day of this kind of thing, even though I was only a spectator under generally favourable conditions: for example, after that day at Darfur I did not go to the state dinner in Khartoum but straight to bed, knowing that my absence in a crowd of two thousand men would never be noticed. The King had to make a quick change and then meet the two thousand, even making speeches to them. His stamina aroused my constant admiration.

From Khartoum back to Jiddah I travelled in the King's plane (a Boeing 720 jet) and made another curious discovery, which was that airmen prefer full fuel tanks when they have heads of states or governments aboard. Khartoum to Jiddah is nothing at all for a Boeing jet—a bit over two hours—but we stopped nevertheless to refuel in the middle of the desert and were disgorged at about noon on March 13th to another cheering crowd at the Jiddah airport.

These days on the Blue Nile and the White Nile and in the western desert may not have been absolutely typical of the King's visits abroad, but I learn from my friends at court that the pattern is much the same. The programme is crowded, the public wild with enthusiasm, the King always gracious, the results uncertain but definite. Let us say that the serious purpose of all these visits is to create an Islamic spirit, a feeling of kinship between the Arab and

Islamic peoples all together. If that is so, surely it is obvious to everybody that the project has been successful. Only the slave press of Nasser, which echoed every order, attempted to denigrate the effect of Faisal's presence in all these countries. It might be said (and Cairo has said it) that the King went to 'reactionary' allies, that such rulers as the Shah of Persia and the King of Jordan are his natural friends anyhow; but how about the liberal Moroccan kingdom and the Left-directed republic of Guinea? Or, indeed, Tunisia which is as 'advanced' in ideas as Cairo ever pretended to be? The uniformity of the response has cemented the notion of an Islam which lies above the ideological disagreements of the hour, and to which an enormous proportion of the Muslim population of the globe owns complete allegiance.

When the President of Turkey referred to Faisal as the 'natural leader' of Islam he was only giving tongue to a truth which all these journeys attest. Turkey, an Islamic country, has been governed by agnostic and laical governments ever since the Ghazi Pasha, Mustafa Kemal, but many of its people remain Islamic, as is shown by the big Turkish contingent at each year's pilgrimage. The joy of the Turkish people at seeing the representative of the Arab homeland, this King of Mecca and Medina, is as significant in its way as the joy that was shown in Persia, the home of the dissident and heretical Shi'a.

And certainly it should be noted that Faisal has never said a word to encourage dissent, dispute or argument on spiritual matters. Of course, according to the beliefs of his ancestors, a good many of his hosts in these late years have been heretical, or at least misguided. The faith as interpreted by the Wahhabi leaves no room for prophets, imams or saints, for incarnations or reincarnations. The "Expected One" will never come.

In the very early days of the Wahhabi conquest of the Hejaz, as we have seen, there were incidents when the aroused desert warriors attacked shrines and holy places (the Tomb of Mother Eve, for example) not because they were what they were but because *all* shrines, *all* sanctified spots which are the locus of special prayer, are forbidden in the Wahhabi. Bleak and austere as it may be, this is the faith of the central desert, in which Faisal was brought up.

How catholic, in the true sense, has been his acceptance of fellowship with those who disagree with him! His journey to Persia was to set the keynote for all that followed. There, in a country which abounds in saints and shrines and all sorts of beliefs, he found it possible to stick to a simple Islamism which aroused great fervour.

Faisal's deep religious feeling, along with his astute intelligence, have here combined in an effort which Gamal Abd el-Nasser could not oppose except by indirection and misrepresentation. If there were to be created or re-created a unified Islamic spirit, whether it centred on Faisal as a person or not, it would certainly oppose the aggrandisement of any Egyptian dictator and the immixture of Soviet Russia in the affairs of the Arab world. Such things are intangibles; too often we count them out; but history has shown how great their power can be in a crisis.

I cannot leave the subject of Faisal as foreign minister, or his judgment in foreign policy, without reverting once more to that luncheon he attended at the White House on, I believe, September 25th, 1962, just after the Egyptian troops had invaded the Yemen.

President Kennedy asked him about these events and the 'republican' regime in the Yemen. The King, who was then Crown Prince and Foreign Minister and had been attending the United Nations General Assembly, replied that there were no republicans in the Yemen; there were factions; the Egyptians had backed a certain faction and had for their own purposes invaded the country. He warned the president, quite solemnly, against recognizing the 'republican' regime in the Yemen. (I have heard the same from Americans who were at that lunch.)

Mr. Kennedy was no doubt impressed; Faisal is a most impressive person. The president did not recognize the 'republican' regime in the Yemen for some time—but he did so in the following January, and the Americans have been regretting it ever since. The situation by which an Egyptian army attempts to annex the Yemen by imposing on it a puppet regime has been systematically opposed by Faisal, usually in the form of supplies to the patriots opposed to the invasion. Unlike Egypt, he sent no troops of his own into the conflict. He is essentially a man of peace. But he knew from the moment of the Egyptian invasion that this was a danger to the independence not only of the Yemen but of all Arabia. In this he saw far and clear—as he has done in so many other matters—and has, once more in my opinion, justified his repute as a seer in foreign affairs, a great foreign minister.

7 Faisal, the King

1

FAISAL's accession to the throne was like a quintessence of all his fundamental policies—that is, bold at heart but cautious in manner, with a gradualism and a legalism which avoided many difficulties that might have arisen. To put it in the simplest terms, he could have taken the throne at any one of a dozen opportune moments during the preceding decade—perhaps, even, at any moment—because his support was so strong and his brother's ill-adjustment to government so obvious. He did not do so. He waited until it became a necessity, and then did what needed to be done with the utmost dignity and decorum.

He was recalled to Arabia and to power after the Egyptian invasion of the Yemen in 1962. In this great crisis the kingdom found itself low in financial reserves as it had been since 1958: King Sa'ud had spent millions on palaces and other forms of display without considering the effects upon the Treasury. The actual existence of the country was in danger and it had little money, in spite of a huge (for that area) income.

Faisal set to work as before. But in all probability there came into his head at this time (if not years earlier) the reflection that the work and the responsibility should go together, that King Sa'ud was fundamentally unfit to govern, that the safety of the country demanded another hand, and that for the preservation of the dynasty this new hand could only be that of Faisal himself.

At all events, during the construction of a solid reserve of gold, dollars and foreign currencies (which was quickly enough accom-

114

plished once Faisal had stopped up the grossest of the leaks) and some help to the defenders of the Yemen, all the reins of government came into Faisal's hands. (He has had every important ministry in turn, usually at its formation.)

By the spring of 1964 it had become quite clear that all power was with Faisal: the pretence, even, of Kingship had departed from Sa'ud. We reproduce here a proclamation of all power to Faisal, phrased as a royal decree from the Regent of the Kingdom, which he had just become under two other documents which we shall give. Here is the royal decree of March 30th, 1964, reproduced from Sheikh Hafiz Wabha's *Arabian Days*, passed as official.

We, Faisal, son of Abd el-Aziz es-Sa'ud, Regent of the Kingdom of Sa'udi Arabia,
With the grace of God,
By virtue of:
The Royal Rescript No. 42 of 9th Shawal 1381 H (2);
Article 20 of the Statutes of the Council of Ministers; the decision of the Council of Ministers No. 753 of 17–11–1383 H;
In accordance with the proposal of the Vice President of the Council of Ministers:

HEREBY DECREE:
Article 1. The decision of the Council of Ministers No. 753 of 17–11–1383 H., the text of which is annexed to the present Decree, is hereby approved.
Article 2. The President of the Council of Ministers and the Ministers are hereby entrusted with the execution of the present Decree, which becomes effective on publication.

(Signed) Faisal.

The whole thing sounds quite meaningless unless you realize that Faisal is President of the Council of Ministers (as well as occupying various ministries); that the Vice President of the Council is his brother Khaled, soon to be Crown Prince; that the instructions given by the Regent are in reality instructions to himself to enforce his own regency. This becomes quite plain when we examine two other documents, one from the Council of Ministers (dominated by Faisal and the Royal Family) and the other from the Royal Family itself. The first document, labelled 'Decision of the Council of Ministers', is as follows:

The Council of Ministers:
In its capacity as the legislative body and by virtue of articles 19

and 20 of the Statutes of the Council of Ministers and by virtue of its competence to promulgate laws and amend them;

After studying the present situation and deciding on the need to put an end to all that may jeopardize the stability of the country or constitute an obstacle to its rapid progress;

Having noted the juridical opinion issued on 16–11–1383 H by twelve Ulemas, the Nation's jurisconsults;

Having noted the present health condition of the King, the Ulemas consider that His Majesty is not in a position to carry out the responsibilities of State;

In consideration of the fact that this legal body—in accordance with the legal provisions which safeguard the public interest—has decided that His Royal Highness Crown Prince Faisal will henceforth be responsible for the functioning of all State affairs, both internally and externally, whether the King is present in the country or absent, without having to refer to His Majesty;

After noting the decision taken by members of the Royal Family by virtue of which the present members unanimously decided that His Royal Highness the Crown Prince Faisal should assume all the powers attributed by the law and by custom to His Majesty the King;

By virtue of the Royal Rescript No. 42 of 9th Shawal 1381 H, acknowledging to His Royal Highness Crown Prince Faisal the title of Regent and the responsibilities of the King during his absence and in his presence;

Aware of the heavy responsibilities he has to shoulder in the momentous conditions through which the beloved country is passing at present;

THE COUNCIL OF MINISTERS DECIDES THE FOLLOWING:

1. As long as His Majesty King Sa'ud, son of Abd el-Aziz, remains the Sovereign of the Kingdom, all the duties and attributions, whether legislative, executive, administrative or juridical, acknowledged to His Majesty in conformity with Islamic law and with the prevailing regulations in the country, are transferred to His Royal Highness Prince Faisal, son of Abd el-Aziz, Heir to the Throne and Regent of the Kingdom. His Royal Highness shall henceforth have sole responsibility for assuming the duties and exercising the attributions mentioned above.

2. All the authority attributed by the laws of the country to His Majesty the King in his capacity as Head of State and Supreme

Commander of the Armed Forces are considered by virtue of the present decision as transferred to His Royal Highness Prince Faisal, the Regent. This transfer automatically implies the amendment of existing legislation and particularly articles 8, 11, 23, 37, and 44 of the Statutes covering the organization of the Council of Ministers.
3. His Royal Highness the Crown Prince and Regent is requested to approve the decree as per attached text, in his capacity as Regent.

Vice-President of the Council of Ministers,
(Signed) Khaled son of Abd el-Aziz.

This document, in its turn, was based upon two others, one of which was a declaration by the Ulemas (16–11–1383 H) and the second a decision of the Royal Family based upon it. They are too long and involved to give in full. The essence of the decision by the Ulemas (the wise men, those learned in Islamic law) is that the interest of the country demands a change of power from Sa'ud to Faisal. It is the only one of all these documents which makes any reference to dispute or conflict between the two brothers. It says:

May God be praised and bless His faithful follower:*
In view of the current conflicts between His Majesty King Sa'ud and his brother, His Royal Highness Prince Faisal, which we studied in our meeting held in the month of Sha'aban;
In consideration of the fact that on 16–8–1383 H. we rendered our verdict on these divergencies with the aim of putting an end to them;
In view of the fact that it is clear that our verdict has not put an end to the devergencies;
In view of the fact that these divergencies have become more serious recently and that they have threatened to cause disorder and chaos in the country, with disastrous results which only God Almighty could foresee;

And so on, but with a full recognition (otherwise absent) that the King and Crown Prince have been in disagreement, the learned men decide that King Sa'ud should remain the Sovereign, with all 'respect and reverence', but that all powers of the state be discharged by Prince Faisal in the absence or in the presence of the King and without referring anything to him. The document concludes with a prayer for Muslim unity and is signed by twelve (which is about unanimity) of the learned men of the kingdom.

---

* The Prophet.

Based upon this document the Royal Family issued a decision in the same sense asking Faisal to take over. This royal document is signed by all the important members of the family without exception —that is, uncles, who come first, brothers, cousins and nephews. I shall not give the list of signatures but I have counted them, and they come to sixty-eight, including Jiluwi and other relatives who are not in the direct line of the House of Sa'ud.

The cautious procedures thus sanctified were brought into play seven months later (November 4th, 1964) when Faisal was proclaimed King. Again the Ulema—the twelve muftis—and the princes of the Royal House made their decision and it was put into effect by decree. Since Faisal as Regent was already the source of all power, police, military or civilian, there was no hint of protest. King Sa'ud wanted, on his departure into exile, to go by night and without ceremony, but Faisal insisted on giving him royal honours and seeing him off at the airport. Sa'ud afterwards—in Cairo—only once indulged in open criticism of his brother or of his own treatment. He died in 1969.

2

What tensions and arguments led to the dethronement of Sa'ud and the accession of Faisal we are not to know, at present, in any detail. We know that Faisal's desire for a balanced budget and a control of expenditure ran contrary to the temperament and inclinations of King Sa'ud. Sa'ud, an impulsive man, was likely to go to greater extremes in any policy (foreign or domestic) than his cautious brother. He was openly accused of conspiring to assassinate Gamal Abd el-Nasser in 1956 and yet became an honoured guest of Nasser in Cairo within a decade. Such contradictions are part of the irresponsible nature of his regime, which was lavish in countless respects although it courted bankruptcy in others. (His palace of Nasiriyeh in Riyadh, one of the largest of modern times, is said to have the biggest air-conditioning plant in the world next to the Pentagon at Washington.) Sa'ud's sons amplified his reputation for extravagance by their behaviour at home and abroad. The flood of wealth which descended upon the Royal Family in the 1950's was treated as private property, the absolute resource of an absolute monarch, to be spent at the Royal will or whim. Faisal's ideas of a Monetary Agency and a balanced budget with fixed appropriations for each ministry or agency of the government (including the Royal Family) ran directly counter to Sa'ud's notions of administration: it was inevitable that they should clash, and that the sober and responsible men of the kingdom should side with Faisal. Indeed it is hardly less than miraculous that there should have been a Faisal at hand in the moment of crisis, ready to do what was necessary to save the currency, the kingdom and the dynasty from catastrophe. Without him it is difficult to imagine what might have become of the country after 1962.

The question of an alternative to Faisal's rule is, indeed, seldom considered in Sa'udi Arabia except in the youngest and most advanced circles of students returned from foreign countries. In successive visits I have heard almost nothing of this kind even mentioned. Of course, they say, the dynasty will go some day; the oil will be nationalized; all kinds of tremendously revolutionary things are going to happen; but when? Few things seem solider than the present regime in Arabia. I am told by experts that if Faisal suddenly grants a constitution, which he may do any day now, the voters will vote for those who already lead them. That is, the tribes (who constitute a large part of the population) will vote for their own chiefs, who are their relatives, whom they know and approximately trust. The city dwellers will vote for the clan leaders they already know, who already hold city positions under the Crown. The vote would change nothing: so the experts tell me. In the meantime only a very few people in the country seem to worry about not having the vote or the other appurtenances of western democracy. Representation in a legislature—trial by jury—the right of habeas corpus—so many of the things that are fundamental to life in the west are unknown, undesired, and even unmentioned in Arabia. What takes their place is the Koranic law, which, for all its genius, is yet the code of a desert people of the seventh century and can hardly apply to every circumstance of today. In a code where usury itself is forbidden (that is, where the citizen can neither give nor receive interest on money) it is difficult indeed to see how the Koran can regulate the proceedings of modern banks. It is done; hair-splitting is a legal gift; I do not know how.

King Faisal's conception of the kingship, of the dynasty and of the rights of the people has been evolving through the years and through his studies. He is by no means a simple Bedouin prince with a concept of ownership. We read in Sheikh Hafiz Wabha's delightful book *Arabian Days*, about a certain Sheikh Jabir of Kuwait (brother of the redoubtable Mubarak) who said, in response to a quotation from the Koran about the shepherd and his flock:

'If the duties of a ruler are as you say, what advantages has he over tradesmen or shopkeepers? My own view is that if an Emir is a shepherd and his subjects sheep, he is entitled to shear their fleeces whenever they become too heavy.'

This view, traditional in the East—and not only in the East!—has never been Faisal's. His sense of responsibility to the inhabitants of his country has been shown from early days and has been made more explicit with the passage of time. His great speech of November 6th, 1962, when he resumed power as Prime Minister after his return from New York, contained many statements concerning the duty of the government to the people. There is one in particular which merits recollection.

'His Majesty's Government is of the opinion that the time has come,' he said, 'for the promulgation of a fundamental law for the country, based on the Book of God, the Shari'a of His Prophet and the life of his wise successors. The law clearly sets down the basic principles of government and the relation between ruler and citizen, organizes the different authorities of the state and co-ordinates their relations to each other. It also sets down the basic rights of the citizen including that of freedom of expression, within the limits of the Islamic faith and public policy.'*

To the simplicities of a western mind this would indicate the necessity ('the time has come') for a constitution. I found to my astonishment that this is not the way King Faisal interprets it today. He objected to my use of the word 'constitution' ('Must you use that word?' he asked) and declared that all the safeguards for the citizen and his rights were contained in the Koran. He finds that all legislation for social justice and security are also contained in the Koren and that there is no need for further action in this realm of ideas. The 'welfare state'—not his expression—is rapidly being constructed in Arabia without the aid of constitutional legislation or a democratic and self-renewing structure.

This may be so (I think it is). No talented boy nowadays should be unable to go through the entire educational system of the country, sustained by scholarships, and then perhaps also work abroad in foreign universities. This is a vast achievement in so very few years, and it will in time be extended to the girls as well: a promising beginning has been made. Hospitalization and pensions are at work. The tribal, family and general Islamic structures preclude, according

---

* *Prince Faisal Speaks*, Ministry of Information, Kingdom of Sa'udi Arabia, December 1st, 1963 (speech delivered November 6th, 1962).

to the King, the occurrence of destitution in old age. In other words, all of our complex system of social legislation, as it exists in the West, is not necessary in Arabia and will not be brought into being.

This is in contradiction to the Policy Statement of Nov. 6th, 1962, already quoted, which outlined a wide range of legislation beginning with the 'fundamental law', and taking in schemes of reform in local administration, social and legal judgment. Of all these points—there were ten of them—the final point, abolishing slavery in the kingdom, is the one which (to the best of my information) has been carried out most literally. Slavery was always domestic in Arabia—there were no large plantations or other enterprises for the use of slave labour on a grand scale, as in the United States—and consequently it was not too difficult to bring about its abolition once the resolution was taken. A racial admixture which is estimated at 7 per cent (to be viewed with doubt, like all statistics in this country) is perhaps the chief result of the centuries during which slaves from Africa were regularly imported into the kingdom. That is, 7 per cent of the present population are supposed to be of mixed blood (partly African) but since there is no means of knowing with any precision what the population is, the number must remain in doubt.

It is also quite evident that domestic slaves who have grown old in a family do not have much desire to leave, and for many such in Arabia the abolition of slavery made no difference. For others, there have been agencies established in the Ministry of the Interior and the Ministry of Labour to see that they are re-settled in work. At all events it has never constituted, nor does it now constitute, anything like the American problem in any important particular. There is no racial prejudice in Arabia, for example, as there is no wholesale exploitation of labour, and the worst horrors of the United States have never been repeated in Arabia. The institution of slavery, originating in war—the vanquished were the slaves—had nothing to do with race; many or most of the slaves in earlier centuries were of the same race as the conquerors; many of them became the parents of honoured warriors, scholars and divines. It was, let us say, a totally different institution from the wholesale labour exploitation which was slavery in the United States. This has made it relatively easy to wash away in a few years (first by the prohibition of importing slaves from Africa; then by the prohibition of their sale; then in 1962 by the abolition of the whole institution), something which in most western minds, particularly American minds, looms as a vast social problem. A great nation which has torn itself asunder over this question, and which still is threatened at the very base of its being by the aftermath, may find it difficult to believe that slavery was never a primary danger to the life of Arabia. Granted, the possession of even one slave is wrong from our point of view; but the institution was accepted for centuries and was mild in its incidence as well as involving relatively small numbers of people; it can bear no comparison to the vast and irremediable anomaly of the United States.

It is curious to me, just the same, that even on this point King Faisal showed no desire, when I last spoke to him, to expatiate. He could well have said that the abolition of slavery had gone through smoothly, and in part because it was not really a great problem in Arabia. I expected him to say something of the sort (I had already made my enquiries at the ministries concerned). Instead of this he seemed to brush the whole thing off, as he did others concerned with the Policy Statement of November 6th, 1962, as being matters of detail which could be worked out with lower officials.

The conclusion to which I came in regard to this Policy Statement —so broad, liberal and just in its tone—was simply that the situation as it developed had afforded no opportunity for the full evolution of the plan, if it was a plan, or the hope (which it more likely was) expressed in that statement. Every single one of the ten points required the expenditure of time, money and talent. How can you set up a judicial council, for example, to revise or modernize the structure of the law courts, unless you find the men to fill the jobs and the money to pay them with? There is talent in Sa'udi Arabia, certainly, but not enough to go round for all the countless jobs now being undertaken. ('Shortage of personnel at all levels', was the main difficulty according to my expert friends.) But aside from the search for the right men for the jobs, there came, at the same time as Faisal's Policy Statement, the Egyptian invasion of Arabia at Yemen, and the order of priorities in expenditure was upset. From then until the present day the intermittent war or the precarious truce in the Yemen has constituted the predominant consideration in Sa'udi political thinking because, fundamentally and in the long run, the existence of the country depends upon it. Sustained by Russia and to some extent even by China, Nasser did have it in his power to undertake a career of conquest which might take him far in the peninsula of Arabia. He was on the brink of it and perhaps refrained only through the inherent weaknesses of his regime and some concern over the power of Faisal's state as well as that of Iran.

3

The extent of Faisal's popularity, though it is obviously real and wide, is hard for a foreigner to estimate. That organized *claque* made up of cheer-leaders and trained shouters, such as we saw it in the Fascist dictatorships and in Cairo and elsewhere, that fine flower of modern demagoguery, is unknown in Arabia. The cheers which greet Faisal in the streets, although not hysterical, have the merit of being spontaneous. The benevolence that surrounds him is manifest in the face of many a bearded old tribesman smiling, in a sort of proprietary affection, at his mere presence.

I have been told by a variety of knowing persons (including Anwar Ali, the astute Pakistani head of the Monetary Agency, who knows the King well) that Faisal would never desert his country whatever happened, that he would find some means of serving it even if the monarchy were no more. I have also been told by quite a number of excellent observers that if there were an election for a president tomorrow, Faisal would win hands down over any possible combination of opponents. These things I am constrained to believe— they are in the situation. After all, Faisal is substantially the one truly national figure in the country, and it would be difficult to think of anybody (in his family or out of it) who could dispute his way. The extravagance of the Arabic press, which, in oriental fashion, never ceases calling him 'The Great' and dwelling upon his outstanding virtues, corresponds in a remarkable degree (or so I am persuaded) to the actual feeling of the people. I have seen him among the people only on a few occasions and, as is common sense, he was surrounded by security precautions, but there is no doubt in my mind that he communicates with them and they with him.

He is not quite as lavish with his time and hospitality as his father was: the conditions of today do not permit that patriarchal extravagance. Even so, Faisal as King is accessible to a very wide range of his subjects—indeed to anybody with a legitimate grievance, petition or appeal. He has fixed days for it (Thursdays in Riyadh, Saturdays in Jiddah) and the ceremony is brief; the demands on his time are far greater than they were for his father; nevertheless he would not pass over this general reception (or assembly, the word used in Arabic) for less than a compelling reason. If tribesmen predominate in these weekly receptions it is because city dwellers, as a rule, have some simpler way of redressing their grievances; the tribesmen, by tradition, go straight to the King and expect to get a hearing.

In Jiddah the reception is smaller than in Riyadh: the tribes are farther away, they do not often come down to the Red Sea, and they do not (as a rule) feel at home in the coastal city. In Riyadh, their ancestral capital, they are much more in natural surroundings; they have lesser distances to go to see the King; they are at home. Consequently the gatherings in Riyadh every week are large. They take place in the palace of the governor (another brother of the King's) in a huge, almost square hall with, on its immense floor, one of the biggest rugs I have ever seen. The King drives there from his own offices across the city. There is a guard of honour of Bedouin sheikhs wearing their swords, most of which are encased in beautiful damascened scabbards of gold or silver (or both). This honour guard makes a sort of avenue through the enormous room to where the King sits in a throne-like gilt chair, flanked by the learned men and notables, with the Grand Mufti (the Mufti of Riyadh) on his right. The tribesmen and others who wish to speak to him, sometimes with petitions in hand and sometimes without, march up through the glittering scabbards of the tribal guard and bow before him. It is customary to kiss hands, but the last time I was present at this ceremony an official warned each petitioner, as he came up, to take the King's hand without kissing it, and this was (with some surprise, I think) obeyed. The protocol officer who accompanied me explained that the King favoured a gradual diminution of ceremony, and thus would dispense with the hand-kissing.

I have never seen Faisal engaged in any very lengthy talk with his petitioners, but he does speak to them all and listens to them as much as time permits. The ancient tradition of Islamic kingship, akin to the Latin 'first among equals', is thus visibly enacted at stated intervals throughout the reign, bringing to life a relationship which modern times seldom can perceive. How much of this is effective democracy, how much tradition, how much a symbolic form, the foreigner cannot precisely determine, but it seems to be a little of all three.

The King is accessible to his subjects in numerous other ways, of course, of which the written petition is perhaps commonest. No insistent visitor with a cause to plead is lightly turned away. I have heard dozens of stories about students, for instance, who obtained the King's favour by stating their cases to him directly, seizing any one of the opportunities offered by his comings and goings. A petroleum expert and organizer of high present rank owes his advanced training (in the United States) precisely to such an audience, in which he showed the King that his academic rating justified a scholarship abroad.

They say that Faisal has never lost his command of tribal dialects (his liking for Bedouin poetry might have helped in this). Nor does he forget the desert trails and the interrelationships of the tribes. It is said that he can argue local geography with the best of the Bedouin and hold his own. In all this, although he has neither the sweeping joviality of his father or the *camaraderie* that often distinguished his elder brother, he is in a give-and-take relation with the tribesmen which concords with the tradition. They habitually address him, I am told, as 'Faisal son of Abd el-Aziz', which is the language of the desert rather than the language of the court.

A very small minority of Western-educated Arabs may dissent from the chorus of praise which surrounds Faisal at all times. Rather, let us say, they do not think this chorus of praise is healthy; they think they should be allowed to criticize the King and his government; they have not many or deep causes for criticism, perhaps, but they would like to exercise that right or, if it be so considered, privilege.

In this matter I do not think the ordinary Arab has any complaint. Free speech or not, he usually says what he wishes to say in private conversation, and I am told that public utterances bore him, the press does not appeal, and only the news—the actual 'hard news'— on the radio is of any particular interest. Radio is everywhere, and any attempt to censor what the public hears would be useless. Radio Cairo, for instance, is freely heard throughout Arabia, and often used to contain bitter attacks upon King Faisal. Even the Israeli broadcasts from Tel Aviv are heard, and they do, I am told, quite a few skilful broadcasts in Arabic.

Under these circumstances it would seem worse than useless to maintain news censorship at all. In fact the Policy Statement of November 6th, 1962, referring to Islamic law as the basis for the projected fundamental law, says, 'It also sets down the basic rights of the citizen including that of freedom of expression, within the limits of the Islamic faith and public policy.'

What these limits may be, of course, no foreigner can judge, but the statement at any rate recognizes freedom of expression as being a 'basic right' of the citizen.

The surprise, then, is all the greater to find that the local press in Arabic is muzzled and that foreign newspapers (those from London and Paris chiefly) arrive on the news-stand in Jiddah with gaping holes where once were news articles of interest to this part of the world. Such items during recent years were chiefly those referring to the war in the Yemen between royalists and republicans, speeches made in Cairo, attacks upon King Faisal and news of the area regarded as dubious or generally unfriendly. (This includes any mention of Israel in ordinary times). The fact is that these foreign newspapers have an extremely limited circulation—not many copies are for sale—and could make, practically speaking, no difference to public opinion among Arabs. The Arabs are really influenced by what they hear on the radio, and radios are everywhere; moreover, they can pick up almost anything in the air without inconvenience or police interference. They hear far worse things from Cairo than they could ever possibly get out of the London *Times* or the international *Herald-Tribune*, and yet these papers quite often reach the news stand riddled with holes.

There is much to be said on all sides of the question, and certainly all countries use censorship in time of war: Sa'udi Arabia was so concerned in the fighting in Yemen that perhaps it might have been considered a party to that war, and of course the war with Israel has never ended. A case can thus be made for censorship. But if so, it should be made for a logical, intelligible censorship, not the self-contradictory system in operation today. All the alert and interested part of the citizenry knows (by radio) exactly what is going on and the speed with which news travels by word of mouth is quite phenomenal. The fixed hours of news and comment from the powerful Cairo Radio are known to everybody and the Friday commentary by Mr. Mohammed Hassanein Haikal, although read by somebody else, had a huge audience for years.

In view of all these circumstances one can hardly regard the censorship as an efficient control of information, thought or opinion in Arabia. It serves, therefore, as an irritant to the alert and interested citizens, inhibits the growth of a natural, native press, and cripples the nation's own radio, without effectively suppressing the news or even delaying it much. Friends have told me the King is dissatisfied with it, but so far nobody has provided him with a substitute arrangement that suits the situation.

A 'political class', as you might call it, scarcely exists in Arabia. The nearest thing to it is the office-holders, who are indeed aware of every change in the situation. There seem to be few citizens outside the ministries and government agencies who take any sustained interest in public affairs or foreign politics. A more steady interest beats upon appointments and promotions, as in all bureaucracies old or new, and along with this is an awareness of what happens particularly in the Arab world, say at least from Tangier to Aden, and of what is said or done in Cairo. Farther afield, say France or England or particularly the United States, is really outer space.

Through this twilight of the old consciousness and dawn of the new, walking like a sovereign and speaking like a judge, Faisal makes his way amidst an admiration which can practically be characterized as universal. His immense dignity and unfailing natural charm have vanquished international gatherings and rallied the support even of Arabs who do not wholly agree with him. Every year, at pilgrimage time, he becomes a kind of centre for Islam, a living symbol, and as time passes this tends to be true on a widening scale during the intervening months between pilgrimages. No such King has been seen in Islam for centuries, and both at home and abroad his very being is an element of power, as well as of relative novelty, in the world situation.

8   The Flare in the Night

1

THE Six-Day War (June 5th–11th, 1967) between the state of Israel and its neighbours, which is called the 'June War' in most Arab references, was blazing proof of the superiority of the Israel army and air force over those to which it was opposed. This superiority came from intensive, single-minded training and preparation for a minimum of twenty years (and, I should say, for the two preceding generations), as well as of magnificent equipment provided by the United States, France and Great Britain. It seems doubtful to me that any country has been so totally militarized, so obsessed with war, as the small state of Israel. It could hardly be otherwise: the Zionists came into Palestine, from all the ends of the earth, with the sovereign idea that they must get rid of the inhabitants, by whatever means and at whatever cost, so as to set up in that restricted area an independent Jewish state for the 'ingathering of the exiles', as they have proclaimed so often. The 'exiles' are the Jews of the whole earth, estimated at fifteen million in number, and in the half century since Zionism came into official recognition with the Balfour Declaration (1917), in spite of every device known to man, no more than two and a half million Jews have been brought into the country. In spite of every effort at extermination in various guises, the Arabs will not all die or go away, and at present number over a third of the population even under Zionist rule. Short of wholesale massacre it is impossible to think of any way to dispose of them.

The Six-Day War was exceedingly brief and dramatic. It aroused lyrical outbursts in the press of the United States and most other

Western countries because of its swift success. The news was liberally seasoned with scornful remarks about the Arabs and admonitions to their leaders (the dispatches of Mr. James Reston to the New York *Times* are a brilliant example). The Zionist forces had no trouble at all in taking on, according to plan, the Egyptians first, the Jordanians second and the Syrians third. The Arabs (as in 1948) had no unified command and no war plan at all, aside from their general half-formulated notion that Israel must go. Troops assigned to the war from many countries never got anywhere near Palestine before it was all over. Israel is (or was) compact and solid, having driven out so many of its native inhabitants in the preceding decades, whereas the Arab countries, except the immediate neighbours, were scattered over thousands of miles. Algeria, for example, had no time to move; Iraq could not get there in time; and Sa'udi Arabia had to send its contingents over hundreds of miles of trackless desert. The technical *and numerical* superiority of the Israel forces was beyond dispute from the first hour of combat. The numerical superiority arose, as in 1948, from the ability to concentrate a maximum Zionist force at a point (one after the other) where the Arabs were inferior. With great skill and brilliance the Israeli forces were swung from right to left of their small perimeter while the Arab reinforcements were still trudging through the desert.

This does not apply to the Egyptian army, which was in force at Sinai but was quickly overcome, as in 1948 and 1956. The air force (which was smallish but good, of Soviet creation) was wiped out by a very simple device: the Israeli planes went out to sea and approached from there at such low altitudes as do not register on the radar screens. The Egyptian air force was destroyed on the ground, like the Americans at Pearl Harbour and at Clark Field in the Philippines, without ever striking a blow. Panic set in and that army was in flight when the Israeli command turned to its other neighbours and administered the two final defeats. By the end of that spectacular week the Zionists were in military control of six times as much territory as had belonged to the state of Israel (if it did belong!) the week before.

This territory, needless to say, was part of the plan and it was extraordinary to see, during the weeks, months and years that followed, how grown-up, educated men in the United Nations went on passing resolutions ordering the Zionist forces to withdraw from them. I never for one moment expected the Israeli army to give up any territory it had seized. My own experience of the Zionists—many of whom were my friends at one time, until I understood better—is that they are fundamentally opposed to any arrangement with the Arabs (or with anybody else) which does not give them the freedom to do as they wish. I know of only once in the past fifty years when they have withdrawn from anything they have seized. It was in 1956 when General Eisenhower, then President (thank God!) stubbornly insisted, over and over again, that they must withdraw from the territories they had taken in the Suez conspiracy with England and France—the last gasp, let us hope, of nineteenth-century imperialism at its shabbiest. Such men as Eisenhower, simple, no doubt, but honest and true, seldom achieve the highest offices in the United States or anywhere else.

At the present moment there is nobody in the Western world who dares to say a harsh word to the state of Israel, no matter what it may do or say. The situation is well understood and every advantage is taken of it. General de Gaulle was permitted his mild criticisms (accompanied by an embargo on aircraft already purchased) because the Zionist rulers, as astute as any in existence, knew that 1968 was his last year in power. They may even have helped to make this come to pass—it has been suggested in France, although not, I think, with any weight of evidence. The power of Zionism lies chiefly in the United States, where not only the Jews, but the non-Jews as well, have been deluded into thinking that this form of colonial imperialism is of angelic origin and must be supported regardless of principle.

The Arabs are thus left with only one friend among the rich and great, which is the Soviet Union.

One sometimes wonders exactly how the Soviet Union came to occupy this position. It was never Zionist at any point, of course—its fundamental beliefs are international, not national, and the idea of creating a *new* nation in a world already cursed with too many was anathema to Lenin—but it was certainly not pro-Arab at any point up to the 1950's. I remember one speech of Gromyko's out at Lake Success in the late 1940's, before the grand simulacrum moved its blue glass bureaucracy to Manhattan Island, when the Soviet Foreign Minister made an extremely cautious acknowledgment of something which he called 'historic rights' of the Zionist idea in Palestinian Arab territory. I sat there (in some seats provided for us by the prime minister of the Lebanon, Faris el-Khouri) with Azzam Pasha at my side, Azzam the founder and secretary-general of the Arab League. We were stunned into wakefulness—a rare thing in those surroundings. Never before had any disciple of Marx or Lenin acknowledged 'historic' rights of this kind—indeed, the very idea is anti-historical, since the same sort of reasoning would put the Arabs back in Spain and the Amerindians in Washington. Gromyko subsequently toned down this acknowledgment, and the word 'rights' became edulcorated into the word 'interests'. I do not know offhand how this goes in Russian, but I do distinctly remember how I heard it both in English and in French.

I was put in mind of Chaim Weizmann, that great and good man whose life's dream had been the state of Israel, and who actually lived to see it come true. Weizmann (a benevolent friend who perfectly understood my inability to dream along with him) once told me about a conversation he had with that supreme lunar module, Neville Chamberlain, along about 1940 when the Nazis were about to attack both Poland and western Europe. ('We must make war while we are still young enough', Hitler had said to Mussolini at Berchtesgaden only a few weeks earlier.) Dr. Weizmann told me that after their talk, which had not been very satisfactory, the prime minister had walked with him to the door and tried a little touch of *bonhomie,* of comradeship and good humour. (Not really his vein, I should have thought.) 'Well, you know, Dr. Weizmann,' says Mr. Chamberlain jocularly, and one can imagine the dig in the ribs whether it occurred or not, 'if you ever do get your Jewish State it's going to be a Communist one, isn't it, ha ha!'

Weizmann, telling me this in London under the bombs a few months later (I used to go to dine with him at the Dorchester Hotel, ending up almost always in the air raid shelter, and he would say to his wife, in his matchless *basso profundo*, 'Vera, remember, *no Zionism!*') laughed from the depths.

Well, of course, Communism and Zionism have practically nothing in common, but it is astonishing to what a degree they have been muddled up in the minds of persons who, like Neville Chamberlain, were accustomed to think in set patterns, inherited frames of reference. Many men who played a part in the history of this century thought because there were a number of Jews among Lenin's collaborators that his was to some degree a 'Jewish' movement. I knew a Russian grand duchess who appealed to the leading synagogue of London to help her when her husband was condemned to death in the fortress of Sts. Peter and Paul in Leningrad (George Mikhailovitch). I have been reliably informed, by a younger member of his family, that the late Kaiser Wilhelm II had these same delusions, and if so he must have received them from Ludendorff, primarily responsible for the 'sealed train' which carried the Bolsheviks from

Switzerland to Russia. The sheer ignorance of individual characters in high positions always startles those who come afterwards (we all know so much more than our parents did!) but we make allowances for royalties; what really does surprise, even now and even me, is that men in practical politics, such as Neville Chamberlain, could be so miserably uninformed.

At all events the deviation of the Soviet Union towards any kind of bow towards Zionism was brief. For the most part the recruiting of young Zionist immigrants to Israel has been forbidden (with more or less severity during the various epochs) inside the Soviet Union, and the Zionist organization in its fully acknowledged public capacity does not exist there. This may be easily understood from any Hegelian, Marxian or Leninist point of view. But that further step, by which the Soviet Union became an actual champion of the Arab cause in the 1950's and ever since, is somewhat more complicated, and concerns the neo-colonialist and neo-imperialist rivalries, ambitions, velleities; it mystifies even its beneficiaries at times; it is not altogether welcome to the regimes of the so-called Left ('Arab socialism') and is deeply suspect to the regimes of the so-called Right (our King and his fellow-monarchs). In short, Gamal Abd el-Nasser would seem to have been the one and only whole-hearted puppet, if puppets have hearts, that Russia possessed in the Middle East, and if I had any part to play in the upper regions of the Soviet Foreign Office and Defence Ministry, I should never have depended upon it.

Permit me, here, to distinguish very sharply between the interests of those two offices. As we have seen earlier (and plentifully!) the British Foreign Office and the India Office were frequently at odds in the affairs of Arabia up to the independence of India (1948). The Foreign Office took the Red Sea (technically, as of Ottoman imperial jurisdiction) and the India Office, or more precisely the Government of India in Delhi, took charge of the Persian Gulf and its region up to Kuwait, including Persia. This cumbersome and at times nefarious division has a sort of shadow in the relationship which now exists between the Soviet Foreign Office and its Defence Ministry. The Foreign Office (like most others in this world) tends toward caution and a limitation on exact engagements, a diplomacy known through the centuries and bearing little or no relationship to the fundamental theory of the Soviet state. The Defence Ministry, which actually supplies tne 'hardware' (a repulsive expression from the Pentagon in Washington) and the instructors on how to employ it, with a fairly wide latitude on the meaning of instruction, has quite different interests. From what I have been told, this department is most keenly and vividly concerned with the actual performance of the machinery (aircraft, artillery, tanks and the devices for the detection of electro-magnetic anomalies in the air or the sea) which has been so lavishly supplied to Egypt since June, 1967. One characteristic of the experts and engineers sent to Egypt in past years has been a certain im-patience with their pupils, and it is no cause for surprise. (It pro-duced dire results for Russian interests in China, for example.) I have been told some weird stories about Egyptian incompetence and Russian impatience. At the same time the Russians are actually curbed by their own Foreign Office to a degree many westerners might not credit. Living all in a heap as they did (I frequently visited that vast Russian compound on the Nile, in my vain quest for a visa to go to Russia with President Eisenhower in May, 1960) there is no possi-bility of an independent life—they are about as free as nuns or monks in the most severe Catholic or Buddhist orders—and they are all in terror of the possible telegram from Moscow. Consequently the Foreign Office, which is a distinctly senior service even in the Soviet Union, suspected of occult information and extraordinary powers, can curb an engineer or a scientist without blinking. It has the highest power there is in Egypt, which is the ability to speak bluntly to any dictator.

One other distinction between the two Soviet services which has come to my ears may be worth a mention. It is that the technicians, engineers and military theoreticians are all a little bit disgruntled at the very bad showing the Egyptians made in June, 1967. They do not believe that their beautiful aircraft ought to have been simply des-troyed on the ground, or that their fine tanks should have been captured in such large numbers—abandoned, many of them, by their Egyptian crews as they fled in panic to the west. The Russians know that their capacity to detect anomalies in the magnetic universe known to us (or within our reach) is almost equal to that of the Americans. They may not actually be able to read Mr. Nixon's thoughts yet but they are not far off it. Consequently it is galling, to say the least, to have their best 'hardware' either smashed to bits or captured by these unleashed Zionists in a few days, only to be sold afterwards to the fourth and fifth categories of European and Asian tribes (without spare parts).

The technicians may not count for a great deal in immediate debate with their own Foreign Office. I have heard that they always lose. But in the long run they count more, because the future is in their hands. The day will come when their voice predominates, and I dread that day. 'Nuts-and-bolts', we used to call them when I was in the United States Army Air Force, those calm, knowledgeable fellows. So long as the mechanism worked they cared not at all, not one single measurable breath, what was underneath it. I have actually been on bombing raids when the pilot commanding (once it was a B-17 in Sardinia, once a B-26 in the Rhineland) asked me what it was that we were dropping our bombs upon. The boy did not really care—he only had a mild academic curiosity. His mistake was in thinking that I knew, because of my advanced age, but it takes something more than age to read a map.

A map, of course, is what the Arab East is to most western people. The New York *Times,* for which my respect plummeted during the Six-Day War of June, 1967, printed maps galore during that week and those which followed, all showing how the armies commanded by General Moshe Dayan had successively defeated the raw levies of Egypt, Jordan and Syria, being immensely superior at each successive point of attack. There was brilliance of command, obviously, and great good luck (the weather on the first day was the prime example of this). There was also the life-and-death devotion with which those who served the Israeli army—mostly made up of reserves, although eminently trained and equipped—went into battle. The state of Israel is a staggering failure when it comes to persuasion, since it cannot 'gather in the exiles' as it aims to do; but those whom it has 'gathered in' are obviously there to live or die. That is what one felt to be a really penetrating truth. I am, was and always shall be *viscerally* opposed to the state of Israel as an unnecessary, belated and inhuman experiment at the expense of the inhabitants of the Middle East. How otherwise decent Americans (such as Eleanor Roosevelt, for example) can have supported such a concentration camp for so many years is beyond my comprehension. It was the only point upon which she (and so many others!) agreed with Adolf Hitler, who was not only a Zionist in the highest intensification, but was in fact the principal artisan of the state of Israel. Without his fateful trajectory across our time that state would not have come into existence.

The Russians, theoretically, ought to consider that the state does not legally, morally or intellectually exist. Even so, they have on several occasions said that they consider it to be in being. They obviously regard it as some kind of American satellite, since its very life is a species of American charity or generosity. (Many good-hearted Americans, both Jewish and non-Jewish, since among us there is not much difference, give money annually to the 'United Jewish Appeal', thinking this to be hospitals and homes for the aged poor, whereas in reality a lot of it goes to killing Arabs in a far-off land where no Jews have dwelt for thousands of years). The Russians know this, as indeed they know everything on the subject. They also know (which the Americans in high office do not) that the state of Israel is not in the very least sympathetic to the doctrines, policies and purposes of the United States. The principal bulwark of capitalism (however modified) in this time is the United States, and the state of Israel is not only non-capitalist and anti-capitalist, but is individually composed of elements which would long ago have chosen the patronage of the Soviet Union if it had been possible. The numbers of Zionists who used to be Communists, and of Communists who used to be Zionists, would astonish both the government in Washington and the New York *Times*. There is no astonishment at this fact in Moscow.

All these reflections swept upon me, as they have done from time to time for forty years, during the 'Six-Day War' of June, 1967. I happened to be in New York at that moment and listened quite carefully to the debates in the General Assembly of the United Nations. The statements made by the Soviet Union seemed to me, from a long knowledge of the subject, pretty extreme. (I doubt if they would stand any test of scholarship.) Even so, they were far and away superior to those made by the Israeli and American representatives. The Russians said and repeated and have never budged from the statement that the state of Israel was the aggressor in the war. I think it is true. It is equally true that the closing of the Straits at the bottom of the Gulf of Aqaba provoked this attack; it is obvious that Gamal Abd el-Nasser was boiling for battle; he said so; and it is also true that Israel had no rights of any kind, legal or moral or international, in the Gulf of Aqaba, in which its single port, Eilath, was seized by force against international admonitions.

And indeed one of the main lessons of this 'Six-Day War' is that the state of Israel does not intend, now or at any future period, to obey or even to be polite about the opinions of mankind. If you have the secure control of New York, Boston, Philadelphia and Chicago, arranged by astute combinations with the Irish, the Italians and the Negroes, what do you care about the moral suffering of the human conscience? When did any of these minorities show any concern for right or justice? What does 'democracy' mean to most Irishmen, Italians, Negroes or Zionists? It means, plainly, a set of political advantages (voting and office-holding and the like, all legal) along with some extra-political and mostly illegal embellishments in the way of contracts for sewage or construction. To these minorities 'democracy' applies only to themselves. The state of Israel, extolled throughout the United States as an example of 'democracy in the Middle East', is in fact a total contradiction to democracy in any form. It proclaims the right of millions of strangers to come into the Arab world and create there an imperial and colonial regime without limits. To the native inhabitants the Zionist organization has so far offered three alternatives: death, exile or slavery. Would the inhabitants of Illinois, Devonshire or Normandy accept these alternatives? Obviously not. Then why do they expect and declare that the Arabs should do so?

One clear response came out of the 'Six-Day War'. It was that the Jews are in some way or manner a superior race (a 'chosen people') with a perfect right, a God-given right, to exterminate or enslave any who get into their way, and that any who dispute this right are sunk in a moral depravity too abject to be contemplated from Washington. This is not really a Jewish point of view: it comes mostly from non-Jewish 'intellectuals' and will be found in our leading newspapers for a few more years, but not for very long, since the events will dispose of it. The Jewish intellects known to me (a few there were) would pause between a shrug and a sigh and perhaps (hastily concealed) a furtive tear. I think of Albert Einstein, on the back porch of his house in Mercer Street, in the town of Princeton, while he waited for me to overcome the difficulties of getting there, and covered (not really covered but sketched) a series of formulae in large symbols, so large that no single page could have contained more than two equations, which I gazed upon—spread out as they were on the table in a splendid fan—and gazing, touched his hand and said: 'What things!' And this old man said to me in his gentlest voice (Mahatma Gandhi's was the only voice I ever heard that was gentler or kinder): 'They are nothing. It was only to pass the time.'

2

King Faisal was on a state visit to Europe when the war between the state of Israel and its three principal neighbours (Egypt, Jordan and Syria) became a reality. Of course there never has been any peace between the Arab countries and the state of Israel, but the perpetual war does occasionally simmer and smoulder. In the ineffable language of the New York *Times* it 'dies down'. At this point, late May and early June, it had 'died down' until it was brought to life again by the oratory of Gamal Abd el-Nasser, dictator of Egypt. This man, who was historically useful in some respects in spite of everything, began to ride the high horse. He was at every point of his career a stupid man, aggrandized by his own egotism and luck, until a handful of Russian aircraft and tanks gave him the notion that he could sweep up the Middle East, sling Israel into the sea and swallow the Persian Gulf. This was not the way it turned out.

If there are any still left who believe that Nasser either had a mission or was capable of one, they are recommended to read his book *The Philosophy of the Revolution*. They could also read his speeches in 1956, at the time of the Anglo–Franco–Israeli conspiracy over Suez, in which he gets the Pyramids and the Suez Canal gloriously confused, or some of his subsequent effusions. One of my favourites was a speech at Alexandretta in 1960 (I happened to be in Cairo at that time or I could never have known about it.) For local reasons this shrewd but uneducated adventurer chose to insult Saint Louis (Louis IX of France) for his Crusade and for all Crusades, and the attack upon Christianity which followed was crass, crude and funny. Perhaps it drew wild applause from those among his audience who understood it; the Cairo newspapers certainly said so; but my own feeling was that I could have done it better myself.

And somehow one always does feel this about Gamal Abd el-Nasser and his so-called mission. The Egyptians are not Arabs and the whole thing was somehow bogus and, implausible. The Arab revival was going along all right before he emerged from that ditch he describes in *The Philosophy of the Revolution*.

Anyhow, he succeeded in provoking the catastrophic Israeli attack of June 5th–11th, 1967, resigned all public office then revoked the resignation and began a frenetical attempt to rebuild the Egyptian army and air force. At the present moment the actual equipment (the 'hardware') is supposed to be better than ever and the Russian instructors more numerous.

Whatever took place in the weeks preceding June 5th–11th, 1967, it is obvious that King Faisal could have had little or nothing to do with it. His relations with Egypt were strained to the utmost by the war in the Yemen. He and lesser rulers around the edges of the Arabian peninsula were shaken by the possibility of an Egyptian advance to the Gulf (and to many of these people the Egyptians, whoever or whatever they are or whatever they may call themselves, are still 'Turks'). The

Shah of Persia was by no means indifferent to the menace, and there is no real doubt that he took a hand in the military evolution, as did King Faisal. How much each knew of the other's activities is another question. What is even shadier, buried in the ultimate penumbra of doubt, is the part the state of Israel played, or might have played, or could have played, in the whole five years of struggle in the Yemen. I have heard many stories and believe none. Since the war of June 5th–11th, 1967, effectively obscured (or indefinitely postponed) any interference in their affairs, the Yemenites have patched things up for themselves and emerged with tribal and local combinations which seem to give some share of power to all the elements save only the remnants of the old royal family. Egypt, Persia and Sa'udi Arabia have averted their eyes, on the whole, because their attention has been so sharply pulled elsewhere. England's retirement from the South Arabian coast in 1968 has not been followed by any startling increase in Soviet power or influence, although that could take place at any time, particularly if the British withdraw entirely from the Persian Gulf. All of these events, so deeply significant to Arabia as a whole and to all its neighbours, are pushed aside by the overwhelming fact that a new military imperialism had arisen in their midst, alien and hostile, which promises them nothing but slavery or death.

Military adventures are no novelty in the Middle East. Conquerors have paraded through the centuries since immemorial time, and not always to the detriment of the conquered. Some mixture or accommodation between nations, races and languages has generally occurred (as it usually did in China) so that after a few decades the ethnographic and social patterns were different and life renewed itself in other forms. Where the conquered are more numerous than the conquerors a process of reverse power comes into play: the newcomer tends to amalgamate with the mass. We always used to hear as a truism of history that the conquerors of China simply, with time, became Chinese, and something of the kind has occurred in other times and places.

But Zionism by its very essence precludes any real adaptation to the Middle East. What led Herzl to his theory of the Jewish state was his People–Nationality concept, under which the Jews of the world, under whatever conditions they live, are aliens to their environment and can only escape that fate by creating an environment of their own. This environment is only to be productive and harmonious (that is, fruitful) in a politically independent, self-governing state. Herzl never thought this invention had to be installed in the middle of the Arab world. It is most doubtful if he even thought such an arrangement desirable, since he was not a religious man and knew little about that Jewish sentiment which annually toasts 'next year in Jerusalem'. He would have accepted any other area big enough for the purpose, and would have 'gathered in the exiles' just as willingly in Brazil or East Africa as in Palestine. What he wanted was a political unit with enough solidity to back up the Jews of Europe in their struggles against the wave of anti-Semitism which disgraced the end of the nineteenth century in even the most civilized countries, such as France. In fact it was the Dreyfus Case in France that caused Zionism to be born in Herzl's mind and instigated his creative work, *Der Judenstaat*. These facts are extremely well-known and have been re-stated even in this very book. Why, then, do the Arabs not know them?

The answer is as simple as night and day. They do not *know* them. They have never been given any intelligible explanation of Zionism, of what it is or aims to be, of what it means to the simple heart of the humblest cobbler in Poland. I believe Zionism to be morally, politically and geographically wrong, but I do not for that reason think it is evil. The Arabs in general, with no exception known to me (and I said *no exception*), regard Zionism as pure, unmitigated evil, a conspiracy against Almighty God and His Prophet Mohammed, upon whom be peace. They are convinced that it is the purpose of the Zionist organization and of the Jews in general (for they never distinguish between them) to destroy the Arabs. I believe this to be a Zionist wish, and have heard it frankly declared, but I do not think it is the reasoned policy of any sane Zionist of this or any other day. The Arabs in general, with hardly any exceptions, believe that the next step in the Zionist imperial programme is to annihilate Islam as a whole, right to the depths of Africa and Asia, including China and Russia, through the demonic wish of the evil forces to destroy the good.

Furthermore, believe it or not (and I can hardly do so myself) the Arabs in general believe that the ultimate aim of the Zionist organization (of which the state of Israel is the dagger and the United States of America the shield) has as its final ambition the dictatorship of the whole world.

It has been my duty to state that these are the things millions upon millions of the world's inhabitants believe. I suppose it is unnecessary to say that I do not.

But I have asked, and must honestly answer, why most Arabs, who are at least as intelligent as non-Arabs and often far more so, should or can or do believe such fantasies.

The very first answer and the one to which I attach most importance is that they hear nothing to the contrary. Of course I know that cabinet ministers, royal princes, ambassadors and other highly privileged personalities can listen to anything they like by means of technological devices the price of which would keep an average Arab family for three years. They can hear whatever lies they prefer and by comparing them arrive at some approximate truth. However, the official versions are those most accessible to the radio and television sets of moderate price. They are also the *only* ones available to radio-television machinery publicly on exhibition, such as those in hotels, cafés or restaurants. To put it briefly, only one version of any fact is normally permitted to go on the air. The same version (in the same words) appear in the next morning's newspapers. It is true that a man of spirit or determination can usually get slightly different versions from his cheap Japanese transistor radio (for which the King's eldest son is the exclusive agent in Arabia), but this would be almost always from Cairo, and—if not—from Baghdad, and what is the difference? Only the rich can afford the B.B.C. and the Voice of America.

What I am trying to say that there is no means by which an ordinary Arab, however much he may yearn for intelligent information, can go about getting it. Censorship is by its very nature not only inimical to truth, but to all information. The two terms cancel each other. If you have censorship you cannot have information.

The second reason why the Arabs have been deprived of any real knowledge of their enemy arises also from the fact that they never realized how dangerous he was. They do not have the benefit of those millions of words every day which recite the achievements of the state of Israel to the equally credulous Americans. They know next to nothing, or did until the June War, about Israel's technological superiority. They thought no Jews could possibly fly aircraft in such a manner, or fight so well on the ground, or manœuvre tanks. The fundamental cause of the Arab belief (still widespread) that the Americans were doing all these things in the 1967 war was that it was impossible to credit the Jews with such accomplishments.

As a result of this slowness to know the enemy (I am still on my second point of Arab ignorance) the surprise of 1967 was total. Until the Arab governments allow their own people to know the truth such surprises will never cease. To prepare any people for self-defence, crusade or vengeance, or indeed for any other form of conflict, the primary necessity is to tell them what they face. This has never been done in the Arab world in modern times, so far as I know. The 'victories' of 1948 and 1956, mostly spewed out by the Cairo radio, were a frightful disservice to all Arabs. When I visited Sa'udi Arabia in 1960 I found a polite and friendly colonel of infantry (who had been deputed to act as my host until King Sa'ud got there) who still believed, after four solid years, that Egypt had won great victories in its war with the Anglo-French–Israeli conspiracy over Suez. The fact that General Eisenhower and he alone (with Foster Dulles at his elbow) quashed that conspiracy and forced the Zionist invaders to withdraw from Egypt was the only Arab victory in 1956, and to this day it is substantially not known to the Arabs what happened.

Nor did they know what happened in 1967. They are never permitted to know; they are never told. The absence of a united command or a plan (any kind of coherent plan) ruined them from the first hour of the war, but they do not know it yet. Perhaps they may have to go through the same experience over and over again before they realize that if they wish to fight a foe in defence of their land they must learn how to do it.

The third reason for the ignorance and confusion of the Arab mind in relation to Israel is that a peculiar form of over-confidence, made up of poetry and legend, has been the only literature aside from the Holy Book itself with which they have real acquaintance. The poems and legends of the desert concern the triumphs of war. This has been true since the centuries before Islam, and although two other inevitable elements (eroticism and mysticism) also surge forth and diminish, they cannot, I am told by learned men, compare in volume or force to the chant of victory, the main theme of tribal song for not only the thirteen centuries of Islam, but long before. These rhythmic chants and dithyrambic recitations, merging into each other so that a foreigner can hardly tell them apart, must be a good deal like the heroic literature of early Greece. Narrative poetry about stirring events of ages past has always delighted men who cannot read, and even some who can; it will certainly set the imagination alight around the campfire for generations of Arabs not yet born.

Now, of course, no Arab ever lost a battle or a war in any of this literature. The victories are incessant, and their interest does not arise out of their results but out of the methods by which those results are achieved. This involves a great deal of what, in western countries, would be called 'boasting', that is, the proclamation of prowess. It goes to the greatest lengths. In examples that have been given me the

Arab hero performs not only prodigies of valour, but also feats which defy the common laws of nature. I do not deny these feats but I am merely wondering how well they prepare the Arab warrior for battle with Israel.

Those are the three main reasons why the Arab world is unprepared for conflict with such a skilful and determined invader. I shall recapitulate them: (1) no government in the Arab world permits its people to know the plain truth about anything important; (2) the Arabs in general have no notion of what Israel is, what Zionism is or what they are up against; (3) they have been nurtured from childhood on a balladry and mythology which by exaggerating their heriosm, prevents them from learning how insignificant heroism is in technological conflict. Any mechanic with a screw-driver and a spark-plug is superior to any hero in modern war, and the Arabs do not know this either.

I have been writing these words, with gravity, with regret and with sorrow, because I believe that the Arabs are right and yet that they have an almost unfailing way of putting their worst foot forward and misunderstanding every result.

The *jihad* which King Faisal has declared against Israel today may not be accepted as authoritative in many parts of the world. (India, Pakistan and Indonesia may all, I think quite certainly, dispute it.) It will, at the same time, carry Muslim Africa with it, and I do not see how it can fail to influence Central Asia, China and Russia, as well as the whole Middle East. Faisal was, in my opinion, swept away by his religious passion.

3

During the days of May and June when the Six-Day War was boiling up and over, Faisal was not in the Middle East at all. His state visit to London was followed by one to Brussels, after which he paused for a brief stay in Geneva, where he maintains a resting-place for just such purposes. There he received General de Gaulle's message from Paris and flew up there for a luncheon with the French president. (France had not been on the itinerary of this journey.) They spoke at some length before lunch and at considerable length afterwards, with nobody else present except their interpreters. There have been statements made in the Arabic press since then which attributed great importance to this meeting.

To shed some light on his attitudes during these critical days one might begin with the dinner given him by the Belgian government at the Town Hall in Brussels when his three-day state visit had ended. At this dinner he attempted to clarify his government's position on 'current events, the nature of which is either unknown or little known in Europe'. (This is May 30th.) The Arabs have been victims for twenty years, their lands taken from them and themselves driven out; the state of Israel, itself a contradiction to the nature of things, has brought all this about, partly on the ground that Jews were victims of Hitler's regime, but we can never accept that we have to pay for that. The Jews have tried to take advantage of the Arab world's division into several states, but this division will not enable them to destroy us, since every Arab, regardless of his nationality is prepared to sacrifice everything to achieve justice.

On June 1st the King met the press in Brussels with all the ambassadors of the Islamic world present. Part of what he said (as published in *Al Safar,* of Beirut) is as follows: 'Perhaps there are those who would convey to the world that the Arabs oppose the Jews *as Jews* but the fact is different. The Jews have lived with the Arabs in Arab countries and generally enjoyed a better life than the Arabs themselves. But when international Zionism came to us with its new policy calling for the creation of a state on the basis of a religious belief we see what we have seen. Since the creation of Israel the Middle East has been continuously in unrest, because the fundamental idea of creating an Israeli state in the midst of the Arab body is an unnatural thing. The Jews were unjustly suppressed during the days of Hitler and the Nazi Party. While we do not agree with the oppression the Jews were subjected to by Hitler and the Nazis, we do not accept in any way that their revenge should be directed towards the Arabs as the Israeli Zionists have shown by usurping a part of the Arab world.'

The King then went to Geneva, where all Arab representatives to the international bodies there (and a number from elsewhere) received him. There was a conference of Arabs from all countries. On the next day (June 2nd) he received General de Gaulle's invitation and on the following day (June 3rd) he flew to Paris to lunch alone with the General. After luncheon at the Elysée he told De Gaulle, at considerable length, what he had already bluntly declared to Harold Wilson in London and to Lyndon Johnson in Washington, that Sa'udi Arabia's policies are no different from those of other Arab countries in this respect; that Arab quarrels are family quarrels and do not constitute any obstacle to Arab unity against Israel; that Arabs everywhere and at every time consider Israel a thorn in the side and that there is no way out except to remove it and give back to the people of Palestine the rights of which they have been robbed; and that, finally, anybody who stands on Israel's side against the Arabs is an enemy of the Arabs.

Faisal arrived at Dhahran on the Persian Gulf (the great Aramco airport) on the evening of June 4th in a special flight arranged with some care by the various authorities, and mostly under military escort in view of the conditions. From the borders of Jordan he was guarded by aircraft of the Sa'udi Arabian Air Force. On the following morning, at dawn, the Israeli attack upon the Egyptians took place.

From June 6th there was nothing but war news on the Mecca Radio, the chief mouthpiece of Faisal's government. It sent out (many, many times, as is the custom in these countries) a message from the King to Gamal Abd el-Nasser in Cairo, with whom his disagreements were well known to everybody, reading in English as follows:

'We stand by your side with all our forces and resources in this fateful battle and we support you in every way. Our armed forces are entering Jordan to work side by side with its Arab sister praying to Almighty God to give us all victory.'

To this Gamal Abd el-Nasser replied (omitting the formalities with which he began and ended), as follows:

'In this battle in which our nation's fate is determined, and in which each of us finds his place beside his brother, we fight together in order to erase the shadow of Zionism from Palestine and gain it back as Arab as it was and as God willed it to be. Our enemy should know that by committing aggression on us they have written defeat for themselves.'

Cables were exchanged with the rulers of Jordan, Syria and the Lebanon as well. There were proclamations in Faisal's name read over the Mecca Radio and in the names of his cabinet ministers as well. The language is a little strange to read years later, considering with what lightning speed Israel was already winning the war. Hardly was the ink dry upon these edicts and proclamations before the Egyptian army was in total defeat and the Zionist forces had turned upon Jordan, the next victim. Sa'udi Arabia, in simple fact, had no time to get into this war at all, and had no remote idea of what was going on until it was all over. 'Victory'—the word 'Nasr'—was in the air, but only in the air.

In fact there was no victory. The defeat was so quick and smashing that the Arabs in general still think it was owing to an intervention from stronger powers than those of the state of Israel. Until they find out the truth (or are permitted to find it out) they cannot fight with any hope of victory, because they cannot even know who is the enemy. They do not in the least realize that the state of Israel is a fact: they still think it to be an invention of American propaganda, which indeed it is in part, but it is also something more.

I have given King Faisal's statements at the time of the Six-Day War to show how firmly he stood with his fellow-rulers of Arab states at that time. Any suggestion of weakness towards Israel on his part is nonsense. He never wavered on that point, whatever his dispute with other Arab rulers may have been. I have talked to him at considerable length through the years and have no doubt. He is anti-Zionist and anti-Israel through and through, whatever may happen hereafter.

9 The Kingdom

SA'UDI ARABIA is geographically so placed, near the centre of the historical world and yet forgotten by it for centuries, that its contemporary course is a product of old forces and new circumstances. Many readers must remember the mediaeval map which Sir Halford Mackinder, in his early days as a geographer of originality, saw on the walls of Hereford Cathedral and took to his being. It was a crude, square map carved in stone, showing the known world with its main line going from Syria to Egypt, and its world-centre, of course, for non-geographical reasons, at Jerusalem. Sir Halford with his fruitful observations on land-mass and the balance of water, the 'heartland' and the rest of it, found that this was not too far wrong for the physical facts of the earth's geography. He felt that the land mass centred somewhere in that region, say in the little area between Jerusalem, Damascus and Mecca, the handful of sand with which we begin this book: it was in any case somewhere between there and Cairo. It lies between the predominant Eurasian continent and the opening world of Africa, an area tiny in comparison to that which it connects (tiny as compared to the North and South American 'islands', too) but momentous in position as it has been in significance to human history.

Mackinder's observations and conclusions fall in part into a theoretical realm where it is not easy to follow him, but what he saw and illuminated in his day was full of suggestion for the future. We cannot help but accept a kind of central aspect, a hingelike importance, for the lands to the east of the Mediterranean, bathed by that ocean and the Red Sea, awakening now to new possibilities of develop-

146

ment through the exploitation of enormous mineral wealth. Air power has made Mackinder's 'land mass' of smaller consequence that he had estimated, and the entire surface of the globe seems to have been drawn in, shrunken, by new inventions of many kinds, but there remains a sense of the vitality of the middle, its potentiality for decision in the affairs of men.

Since at least the first world war—with some adumbrations earlier —there has been going on a series of inner convulsions in all the areas; it is what is called the 'Arab Revolution', taking place in many forms in many states, and augmented by the creation in recent years of the State of Israel, which, small as it is, operates as a perpetual goad on the Arabs and a means of ensuring that their nationalism will not lapse again.

What are the characteristics of the 'Arab Revolution' and how can it claim to be a single movement bringing together aspirations of widely varying content?

It is, first of all, Arab by definition, not Islamic, and certainly not Christian or racial: anybody who speaks Arabic as a native language and accepts or practices the Arab way of life is an Arab according to the definition prefaced to the constitution of the Arab League. Under this meaning all the populations—widely varying in race—from the Atlantic Ocean across Africa and through the Middle East to India (Persia and Afghanistan excepted) may be accounted Arab. Islam is, it is true, larger than the Arab world (much of Asia and Africa is included in it) and an appeal to Islam is always implicit in the great Arab movements even when they do not say so. There is also an important Christian community scattered through the Middle East and North Africa, equally Arab, participating in the literary and artistic developments of the past few decades, and active to a high degree in the Arab awakening. (George Antonius, author of that epochal book *The Arab Awakening*, was himself a Christian; so are Professor Hitti of Princeton and numerous other spokesmen of the modern time.)

In the Arab Revolution as thus conceived there are no barriers of race or religion. A more subtle barrier may be the phrase 'our way of life', so hard to define: it is food, climate, habits of all sorts, clothing and values of almost innumerable kinds and power. A Christian Arab may feel himself to be—gladly and proudly—an Arab in all these respects, valuing the culture to which he is heir; he is therefore, regardless of religion, an Arab nationalist, a true adherent of the Arab League. And on the Left, of course, in the hodgepodge of half-defined parties and movements which have burgeoned in the Middle East for twenty years (in Syria, Iraq, Libya and to some extent in the Lebanon) there are avowed atheists and agnostics, disclaiming all connection with Islam or Christianity either, who nevertheless qualify as true Arab nationalists and legitimate followers of the Arab League.

In race the same catholicity obtains. The African admixture, in particular, has made itself noted in modern time, and some leaders in all countries have shown black African descent to greater or lesser degree. The late Pasha of Marrakesh (El Glaoui) looked African to me; I have met Arab officers in Arabia who seem the same; in Cairo there are numerous exemplars, and I remember one prime minister of the pre-Nasser days who was pure African (Mohammed Mahmoud Pasha). In Islam, effectively, there is no race, no racial feeling, no distinction or prejudice based upon race. As it stands now, on the estimates, the population of Sa'udi Arabia has an admixture of 7 per cent from Africa as against 12 per cent of African origin in the United States.

Against this catholicity there must be set, it is true, the barrier against the Jews. It is based, so far as I have been able to determine, upon the existence of the state of Israel as an enemy intruder (an invader with aims of conquest) in the midst of the Arab world. The Arab states all consider themselves to be in a permanent state of war against the state of Israel, with a blockade and all the rest of the warlike attitudes. The hostility flares up; it can scarcely fail to do so; and although the state of Israel is itself small, it is militarized and disciplined beyond any but a very few in history, and in the whole Arab world there is nothing to compare with it in these respects. In 1948 and 1956, and above all in the Six-Day War of June, 1967, these facts were demonstrated. What a longer conflict might bring—well, it is difficult or impossible to estimate. It would involve too many other elements and forces, including the great powers and the remoter Arab states which hitherto have never been able to participate in the struggle.

The stance of war, in and out of season, is therefore natural to the Arab world with respect to the alien state of Israel in its midst. How could it be otherwise? There are great differences between the Arab states and the Islamic states to which they are allied. In some of them there have been Jewish populations for centuries, living a separate but tolerable and even sometimes privileged life (it was so in Egypt until only a few years ago). There are no non-Muslims normally resident in Sa'udi Arabia because it is a Muslim state; it is so defined; modernity and the oil exploitation have brought in large numbers of alleged Christians (on visas for specific purposes and limited duration). In many respects Sa'udi Arabia may be considered sealed off from the non-Muslim world but, as anybody can see, this is all breaking down, yielding to modern necessities. There is far more coming and going of foreigners to be observed now than there was even a few years ago, and it is relatively easy for the friendly infidel to travel anywhere in the country (except, of course, in the Holy cities of Mecca and Medina).

This being so, what can we make of the fact that King Faisal in March, 1966, speaking at the palace in Khartoum to an audience of international diplomats, parliamentarians and journalists, made an appeal to 'all the great monotheisms' to join in his struggle—or, rather, in the struggle he regards as inevitable—against subversion and chaos in the Middle East?

2

My own guess, only a guess, is that the King looks forward to a time when the barriers of travel for 'the great monotheisms' will be reduced in the interest of some common effort. It is too soon to discuss it or perhaps even to mention it, but the opening up of a once sealed and forbidden kingdom—already on the way—may become an accepted fact before the King has completed his mission.

But larger, much larger than this, is the question of what the King really intends in his highest purpose, that which sends him, as Keeper of the Holy Places of Islam, on so many journeys to the far corners of the earth.

It has seemed to me throughout that his main purpose is simply the defence of Islam—its preservation against the assaults of alien force. He has other purposes too, in which the security of his own country is vital, but any study of his words and gestures must result in a conviction that the defence of Islam always comes first. Perhaps they are indissoluble, and from Faisal's point of view they must be, since Arabia and Islam can scarcely be separated in his eyes; but the larger purpose, the Faith of the Prophet, seems to illumine all.

Close friends of the King have said to me (as I have already quoted) that the calamity of the age is the admission of Soviet Russia and its ideas or practices into the Arab world. This event, the reality of which can scarcely be ignored or its importance diminished, was chiefly the work of Gamal Abd el-Nasser, dictator of Egypt, although kindred efforts have been seen in other Arab states. In the Yemen, where a lackadaisical Turkish suzerainty was succeeded by independence after the first world war, the old Imam (Yahia) was the first to invite the Russian engineers and technicians into his very backward realm; they made the new port of Hodeida and an important road inland to the capital; they made the Egyptian invasion of 1962 possible and did what they could to bring about its success; the Americans and the Chinese, who also were eager in good works in the Yemen in 1960, could not compete with this early advantage. Meanwhile the *coup d'etat* of 1954, in which the old Imam and three of his sons were killed, had left the mountain kingdom with an ailing heir and a royal family which, holding all the high offices, could not compete in external representation (in 'image') with the so-called 'republican' politicians who, under Egyptian auspices, offered a new regime in 1962.

In the years since then much has changed. The Egyptian forces, which at one time numbered about 75,000 men, equipped with Russian airplanes and artillery, have never at any time occupied more than a third of the country, mostly lowland. The so-called 'royalist' opposition, at times heavily supported from Sa'udi Arabia, controlled the rest and was said to engage the good will of most of the people, who are above all anti-Egyptian (anti-Turk, as they say). In addition the Egyptians behaved as conquerors, executed a good many of their puppets, and permitted no real autonomy to the Yemeni in the territory under their control.

Even though it is or seems to have ended, it would be impossible to underestimate the nature of this threat to Sa'udi Arabia as a whole. The Yemen itself is an enclave of geographical and strategical importance; under Egyptian control it would constitute a true foothold in the peninsula. What is more, much more, is that it connects with the former British protectorate of Aden on the elbow of the peninsula and thus with all the numerous other states along the southern shore; and that the British leaving in 1968 saw the Yemeni population, always explosive from the point of view of the Middle East, spreading well into Aden and adjacent territories. It was organized by the Egyptian commissars into pro-Nasser associations and clubs and Mafias of one sort or another, up to now prolific in violence.

The population of the Yemen—estimated nowadays at about three and a half millions, more or less what the lowest estimate is for Sa'udi Arabia—has always been relatively large and relatively anxious to expand. The fertility of the highland valleys and the comparative clemency of weather have no doubt favoured this growth, which from earliest days sent forth a stream of emigrants across the neighbouring sands to wider lands and water. The whole Arab world is supposed to have originated in this way in the Yemeni highlands.

There are actually said to be 120,000 Yemenis registered as residents of Aden at the present time* out of a total population of 280,000.

If the world at large were conscious of the issues there might be no chance for Egyptian ambition in South Arabia. But this is not the case: the world knows and cares little about those remote regions, there are (rightly or wrongly) areas of greater concern to the west, and the whole reality of the Middle East is obscured by western obsession over the fate of the state of Israel. That small state, which could never affect the wider issues, is the only aspect present to the political mind in the west (particularly in the United States), and under that cloak of invisibility it is quite possible that the entire Arab world could pass into the Russian sphere of power without real notice taken, at least until it was too late. The state of Israel, tiny but vociferous, has rendered its neighbours unseen and unheard.

The battle undertaken by King Faisal for Islam, the Koran and the Prophet thus merges very practically into the struggle for his own country's existence, even though it should be without benefit of the world's attention. An identity exists and is profoundly felt between the Islamic realities (which, naturally, are different today from those in the seventh century) and the Sa'udi kingdom as keeper of the Holy Places; King Faisal personifies this recurrent ideal; but he also is the defender of the Arab land, the mother-peninsula, against the invader, and in the most secular and practical sense he stands guard over the rights, privileges and wealth of its people. These are by no means negligible powers and any assailant would be wise to take them into full account.

Yet in the material world men must count in material things. Egypt has thirty million inhabitants and Sa'udi Arabia itself—without allies —has something between three and a half million, the smallest, and seven million, the largest estimate. Egypt has had the advantage of modern Russian equipment in the air and on the ground for more than a decade, with expert advisers and training. The spirit of the troops is another matter; the experiences of 1948, 1956 and 1967 would show that the army was something less than ready for battle.

---

* *New York Times*, March 11, 1967.

However, in 1948 the Egyptian army was deficient in almost every essential supply, and perhaps the episode could scarcely count; 1956 is another matter. In that brief campaign the Egyptians were decisively defeated by the Israeli, and but for the occupation of the Suez Canal (to Ismailia) by the British and French, with its paralyzing effect on the whole world, the campaign might have ended in a catastrophe for Nasser. He was saved by the great powers, who turned his defeat into victory and enabled him to pose as a military hero for a while, but the actual military value of his resources was not then proved—nor has it been proved in the Yemen since then. Whatever the merit of his newly trained and equipped army may be in battle, it has never been shown. In 1967 again it experienced total defeat.

These years may thus affect the course of events in the Arabian peninsula for a very long time. The imperial ambition of Egypt is perfectly clear (there is no attempt to disguise it) but it expresses itself, as did the ambitions of Napoleon, in an attempt to help 'the people' against their oppressive rulers. The representative of Egypt at the United Nations made a speech in this sense to the Correspondents' Club there on March 23rd, 1967, declaring the purpose of his country in no uncertain terms. The fact that 'the people', as organized and made vocal in South Arabia, were financed and organized by the agents of Nasser, operating obviously in his interest, is not supposed to count. The Trades Union Council in Aden, which speaks for Nasser, attacks its enemies (the Federation rulers) as reactionary tyrants, and no attempt at reconciliation has yet yielded any result.

Much might depend upon the attitude of the great powers if they were capable of assuming one. Soviet Russia is deeply engaged in the Egyptian gamble but could swiftly and brilliantly disengage itself from all responsibility if it proved to be dangerous. (This has been seen often). The western powers, effectively England, France and the United States, have been blinded and crippled for years. So long as the Israeli state is the only thing that counts, any number of ruinous blunders may be made in the Arab world around it.

And 'public opinion', which is supposed to govern the great western democracies, plays almost no part in this question at all: that is, it is a cut-and-dried affair from generations ago, not open to discussion, and anything at variance with the wishes of the state of Israel is regarded as intellectually suspect and morally evil. (It is also fatal to the candidate for American office who dares consider it in New York, Chicago, Boston or any other large American city.) The blight, amounting to paralysis, has covered the entire question of the Middle East, and there are countless young or youngish Americans who have never heard a dissident word on the subject. To a very considerable extent—to an extent the fathers of the American Republic would have regarded with horror—the state of Israel has become the 'favourite nation', capable of influencing every relevant decision on the part of the United States and, to a lesser degree, of England and even France.

Now—such are the anomalies of the day—this might not of itself be a bad thing for the defence of Arabia against Russo-Egyptian aggression. It is conceivable that when the critical moment is at hand the state of Israel might do nothing at all—might be dumb, if alert, at the conflict of two enemies. Israel might permit, under such circumstances, the United States to act in the American national interest. These are all suppositions, and must not lead us too far: but the factor of the alien, the relentless stranger, the invader from afar (that is, the State of Israel) can never be more than momentarily absent from an Arab's consciousness. Whether Egyptian or Sa'udi or in fact any other kind of Arab, including those who dwell in Africa, all are the same in this.

There is also the possibility (the direct opposite) that some rash act by Israeli militarism might bring on another armed conflict with the whole Arab world. This, indeed, could unite the Arabs, could obliterate their rivalries for a while and could for the time being obscure those really fundamental antagonisms between the Russian-sponsored states and the modern progressivism of Faisal. But there is little likelihood that any Israeli truly wishes a conflict with all the neighbours at once, who, although always likely to be vanquished in the earlier stages of a campaign, are so far more numerous and wide-spread that it is difficult to forsee any permanent victory over them.

In sum, what we have seen was an aggressive Egyptian imperialism aimed at the Arabian peninsula and its vast mineral wealth, but operating in slow stages. In this process the Soviet Union was in-volved as the patron of an Arab neo-imperialism, as the source of up-to-date arms and equipment in the air and on the ground, and as the ultimate beneficiary of the Nasserian adventure.

3

Against the complications of the time of Russo-Egyptian ambi-tion, the figure of Faisal stood steadfast, wondering at times it seems to me, but unbending and unafraid. I say wondering because I have heard the King express himself in ways which indicate astonishment at the behaviour of those whom he would call 'Islamic brothers' or 'Arab brothers' and who have betrayed his trust. He does not break into vituperation over this—far from it; I have never heard him speak ill of anybody; his anger, which may be felt now and then, is controlled. I heard him trace the entire history of Arab-Egyptian conversations over the Yemen (which is complex) at a press conference in Jiddah once, and those correspondents, almost all from other Arab states, were sharp and persistent in their questions. He was cautious, precise and courteous in all his answers, smiling now and then, taking his time, scarcely ever making a point with impatience or anger. He was equally simple, steadfast and unchanging in a private session (something almost like a press conference) on his visit to New York in 1966, at a time when he was under attack in the press as having declared himself an anti-Zionist. (What else the American press expected him to say, one wonders.)

This man, so far as the judgment of a seasoned observer may go, knows his own mind and purposes and will make his way onwards without essential doubt. He inherited a backward kingdom in the desert and found it to be thundering with riches. Thus he is much envied and gazed upon with some awe by all in the immense region where the Arab tethers his camel (if he still does) or waters his Ford. But Faisal himself has never, so far as I can see, altered his adherence to the Prophet, the Koran and the welfare of his own country. He is not in the least shaken by the vast power represented, in Jiddah or Riyadh, by the Western ambassadors. (There is no Soviet ambassador and the Chinese are only from Formosa.) The idea of Faisal as a 'puppet of American imperialism', is, like so much propaganda, a plain fabrication. He has shown at all times, with respect to the oil companies as to the governments of their countries, a spirit of positive and sometimes awkward independence. They treat him with enormous respect, as indeed they have learned to do by experience. Greatly as they have benefited his country in the past two decades, the fundamental ownership of the land and its resources has never been—and never could be—in question for a moment. He has maintained towards them all (the British, French and Japanese as well as the predominant Aramco, the Americans) a stubborn and haughty regality at least equal to that of his father if not more pronounced. Sometimes there has been a susceptibility in these respects (those of national dignity and *amour propro*) beyond what the westerners expect or can readily understand. In such cases it is normal for the westerners to yield without argument.

Faisal stands, as we see it, for an enlightened traditionalism which hopes to pull Arabia into contemporary existence without sacrificing any of those values which formed his Faith and preserved its essence through the thirteen centuries of Islam. Changes, and very great ones, are in prospect, but none which consist of repudiation of the past or blind adherence to alien and misunderstood doctrines. It is this desire for continuity—the desire to keep development on the rails of history and logic—that constitutes the strength of the King's position in his own world. It would be an absurdity to ask desert Arabs to become Americans (or Russians or anything else) in fifteen years, and the whole power and meaning of Faisal's mission is to see that this shall not occur—that whatever changes may come, and however rapidly, they leave the Arab essentially true to his own nature and heritage.

Now, in that question which most Americans and many Englishmen ask first of all—'is he for us or against us?'—there is little doubt that an alignment of forces, a calling-of-the-roll, would find Sa'udi Arabia on the side of democratic development, although in almost countless questions there might be divergences of opinion. The Sa'udi vote in the United Nations has been anti-imperialist and anti-colonial on specific questions, by and large, going along with the African-Asian bloc in most cases, and we should expect it to continue in that sense. The economic position of the American oil companies in Arabia has nothing to do with the country's foreign policy, so far as one can see, and the precautions taken to ensure that this be so are endless. However many U.N. votes show the Arabs opposed to the Anglo-American combination on specific issues, the fundamental fact still is that Arabia falls on the American rather than the Russian side of the line into which the world is unfortunately divided. This is so regardless even of the great illusion, the living contradiction in terms, the state of Israel: in the larger cleavage in which we may some time come—although most of us think it impossible—that state might take its place as a diversionary episode unrelated to the main stream of human experience.

Finally, the King's mission as he has defined it does not confine itself to Islam or the Arabs, in any patriotic or warlike sense: it aims at peace. That may be far off and difficult to attain, but its possibility is the premise of every religious philosophy known to us, including all of those three which bloomed in the same desert so long ago,

Judaism, Christianity and Islam. Faisal wishes to preserve his own country (with his dynasty or, I think, even without it, although he may regard them as almost identical) but he wants even more to fulfil his own vow to Islam and to humanity.

Events have crowded in upon the limited frame, so small in the beginning, of this brief study. Since 1965, when it began, wars and rumours of wars have obliterated the horizon, not always but often. The war of June, 1967, which I have called 'the flare in the night', was the most spectacular of these. There will be other flares in other nights. Since March, 1969, when it became obvious that no form of negotiation would be possible in the Middle East, the violations of the peace have been more frequent every week. What it amounts to at the present moment is a species of war pretending to be less savage than it is—the murderer with the rose. Every day brings the assurance of worse to come.

In the midst of this darkling landscape the figure of King Faisal stands unafraid. The faith that sustains him is strong, very strong. In the elements of the world struggle this is seldom appreciated or even acknowledged, but it is true. There are countries of whom it could never be said, however much they might temporarily becloud the mind of man. Of Arabia it can be said, as for ages past: it is a constant.

Index

Acknowledgments

The Publishers acknowledge with thanks the source of the following photographs:

Royal Geographical Society
  Captain W. H. I. Shakespear Bin Sa'ud's Army on the March; Riyadh, the Great Street

  N. Mayers Ibn Sa'ud, King of Hejaz and Nejd: King Ali Drives to Prayer
  Captain G. Leachman Riyadh, Great Mosque
  H. St. J. Philby Dari'yah; Hofuf
  W. Thesiger Asir Tribesmen

Camera Press King Faisal at Mecca; King Faisal and the Council of Ministers

Camera Press (Lord Lichfield) King Faisal in the Dwan; King Faisal and Petitioners

Radio Times Hulton Picture Library UN Conference, London

Aramco Library, Dammam King Abd el-Aziz; Ras Tanura Refinery; Dhahran Airport

Aerofilms Jiddah—Mecca Gate

Vincent Sheean The author; the author with King Faisal (back jacket)

All other photographs in this book are the copyright of University Press of Arabia

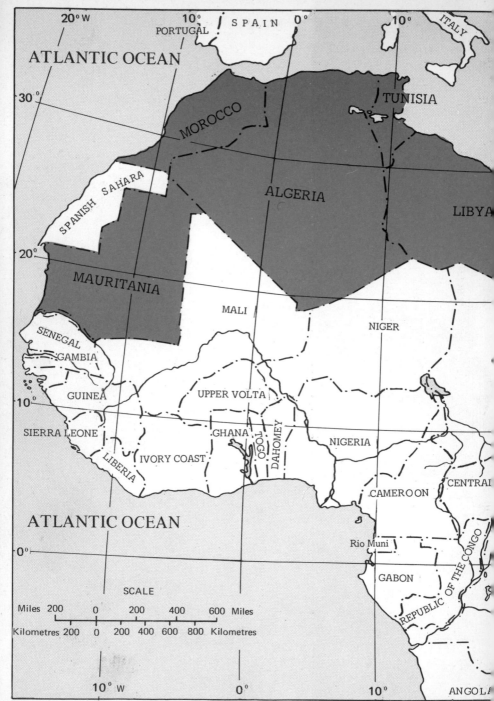

ATLANTIC OCEAN

20° W   10°   SPAIN   0°   10°   ITALY

PORTUGAL

30°

TUNISIA

MOROCCO

ALGERIA

LIBYA

SPANISH SAHARA

20°

MAURITANIA

MALI

NIGER

SENEGAL

GAMBIA

GUINEA

10°

UPPER VOLTA

SIERRA LEONE

GHANA

NIGERIA

TOGO

DAHOMEY

LIBERIA   IVORY COAST

CENTRAL

CAMEROON

ATLANTIC OCEAN

Rio Muni

0°

GABON

REPUBLIC OF THE CONGO

SCALE

Miles 200   0   200   400   600 Miles

Kilometres 200   0   200 400 600 800 Kilometres

10° W   0°   10°   ANGOLA